"*Witchcraft Today Book Two: Modern Rites of Passage* is a book of active leadership that we have been sorely missing. The authors are gutsy and to the point, their words crashing through the shake-n-bake diatribe found in so much of the 'Pagan' material we feed on today. They are not afraid of dealing with modern issues, and you'll not find them sweeping topics like aging, teenage suicide counseling, or grief and death under a sparkling pentacle carpet. *Modern Rites of Passage* is the act of real Craft clergy in motion. These are writers with wisdom and vision who do not fall within the realms of Bambi-Paganism. With this book you can utilize the knowledge from the past to create the religion of the future. No solitary, coven, or clergy should be without it in their library. To teach the Craft of the past, you need the wisdom from the minds of the best practitioners of the present. Here … you have it."

—Silver RavenWolf
author of *To Ride a Silver Broomstick*

"A significant work not only for practicing Wiccans, but for any person interested in religion, anthropology, or psychology. Clifton has succeeded in editing a book whose goal is to help modern Witches create rituals for every cycle of life, from pre-natal to death. However, I also found that this volume illuminated for me the considerations that leaders of any religious organization must go through when creating rituals that will answer the many spiritual needs, questions, and fears of a community, even one as diverse and geographically spread out as modern Witches.

"What also makes this piece timely and involving as opposed to merely scholastic, is that as the inquisitional witch-burning fury of Christianity has slowed over the centuries, modern Pagans are recreating their lost religion within its ubiquity. And as they do so, they find in the pages of this book, communication on how to tread safely within the prevailing mores while maintaining their beliefs."

—Andrew Borakove
Psychic Reader

About the Editor

Chas S. Clifton holds a master's degree in religious studies with an emphasis on the development of new religious movements. He lives in the Wet Mountains of Colorado where he writes about Western esoteric traditions.

To Write to the Editor

If you wish to contact the author or would like more information about this book, please write to the author in care of Llewellyn Worldwide and we will forward your request. Both the author and publisher appreciate hearing from you and learning of your enjoyment of this book and how it has helped you. Llewellyn Worldwide cannot guarantee that every letter written to the author can be answered, but all will be forwarded. Please write to:

Chas S. Clifton
c/o Llewellyn Worldwide
P.O. Box 64383-378, St. Paul, MN 55164-0383, U.S.A.

Please enclose a self-addressed, stamped envelope for reply, or
$1.00 to cover costs.
If outside U.S.A., enclose international postal reply coupon.

Free Catalog from Llewellyn

For more than 90 years Llewellyn has brought its readers knowledge in the fields of metaphysics and human potential. Learn about the newest books in spiritual guidance, natural healing, astrology, occult philosophy and more. Enjoy book reviews, new age articles, a calendar of events, plus current advertised products and services. To get your free copy of the *New Times*, send your name and address to:

The Llewellyn New Times
P.O. Box 64383-378, St. Paul, MN 55164-0383, U.S.A.

Witchcraft Today

BOOK TWO

Modern Rites of Passage

Edited by
Chas S. Clifton

1993
Llewellyn Publications
St. Paul, Minnesota 55164-0383, U.S.A.

Cover Photo by Malcolm Brenner

Library of Congress Cataloging-in-Publication Data

Modern rites of passage / edited by Chas S. Clifton
      p. cm. — (Witchcraft today : bk. 2)
   Includes bibliographical references.
   ISBN 0–87542–378–7 : $9.95
    1. Witchcraft.   2. Paganism.   3. Rites and ceremonies.
 I. Clifton, Chas.   II. Series.
   BF1571.M65   1993
    133.4'3—dc20   93-22967
                                                CIP

Llewellyn Publications
A Division of Llewellyn Worldwide, Ltd.
P.O. Box 64383, St. Paul, MN 55164-0383

Editor's Note

Modern Rites of Passage is the second book in Llewellyn's *Witchcraft Today* series, a series named partly in honor of Gerald Gardner, a founding figure of the modern Craft, whose own book *Witchcraft Today* (first published in 1954) was unique in its time for dealing with the modern religion rather the rehashing the "witch trials" of earlier centuries. The first book in the series, *The Modern Craft Movement*, offered a variety of subjects from sex magick to dealing with government and the news media to being a solo Witch rather than a coven member. Future books in the series are projected to cover the relationship between Witchcraft and shamanism (classical, neo-, and para-) and to deal with the organizational aspects of Witchcraft as religion as well.

As series editor, I would like to thank several people who helped me with this book. Professor Daniel Noel of Vermont College critiqued the introductory chapter and helped improve it. Elizabeth Clifton, RN, CNM, contributed her expertise to the childbirth resource section. Llewellyn's acquisitions editor, Nancy Mostad, helped me through the inevitable delays and arranged for the participation of some of the contributing writers. Mary Currier read all the chapters, made valuable editorial suggestions, and kept my spirits up.

CONTENTS

Principles of Wiccan Belief

In 1974 one group of American Witches meeting in Minneapolis adopted the following group of principles. Since then several versions of these principles, with minor differences in wording, have been circulated. These principles are not required of anyone, but they do reflect the thinking of many modern Pagan Witches whether in the United States or elsewhere.

The Council of American Witches finds it necessary to define modern Witchcraft in terms of the American experience and needs.

We are not bound by traditions from other times and other cultures, and owe no allegiance to any person or power greater than the Divinity manifest through our own being.

As American Witches we welcome and respect all teachings and traditions and seek to learn from all and to contribute our learning to all who may seek it.

It is in this spirit of welcome and cooperation that we adopt these few principles of Wiccan belief. In seeking to be inclusive, we do not wish to open ourselves to the destruction of our group by those on self-serving power trips, or to philosophies and practices contradictory to those principles. In seeking to exclude those whose ways are contradictory to ours, we do not want to deny participation with us to any who are sincerely interested in our knowledge and beliefs.

We therefore ask only that those who seek to identify with us accept those few basic principles.

1. We practice rites to attune ourselves with the natural rhythm of life forces marked by the full of the Moon and seasonal quarters and cross-quarters.

2. We recognize that our intelligence gives us a unique responsibility toward our environment. We seek to live in harmony with Nature, in ecological balance offering fulfillment to life and consciousness within an evolutionary concept.

3. We acknowledge a depth of power far greater than that apparent to the average person. Because it is far greater than ordinary, it is sometimes called "supernatural," but we see it as lying within that which is naturally potential to all.

4. We conceive of the Creative Power in the Universe as manifesting through polarity—as masculine and feminine—and that this same Creative Power lives in all people, and functions through the masculine and feminine. We value neither above the other.

5. We value sex as pleasure, as the symbol and embodiment of life, and as the interaction source of energies used in magical practice and religious worship.

6. We recognize both an outer world and an inner, or psychological world—sometimes known as the Spiritual World, the Collective Unconscious, Inner Planes, etc.—and we see in the interaction of these two dimensions the basis for paranormal phenomena and magical exercises. We neglect neither dimension for the other, seeing both as necessary for our fulfillment.

7. We do not recognize any authoritarian hierarchy, but do honor those who teach, respect those who share

their greater knowledge and wisdom, and acknowledge those who courageously give of themselves in leadership.

8. We see religion, magic, and wisdom in living as being united in the way one views the world and lives within it—a world view and philosophy of life which we identify as Witchcraft, the Wiccan Way.

9. Calling oneself "Witch" does not make a Witch—but neither does heredity itself nor the collecting of titles, degrees, and initiations. A Witch seeks to control the forces within her/himself that make life possible in order to live wisely and well without harm to others and in harmony with Nature.

10. We believe in the affirmation and fulfillment of life in a continuation of evolution and development of consciousness giving meaning to the Universe we know and our personal role within it.

11. Our only animosity towards Christianity, or towards any other religion or philosophy of life, is to the extent that its institutions have claimed to be "the only way" and have sought to deny freedom to others and to suppress other ways of religious practice and belief.

12. As American Witches we are not threatened by debates on the history of the Craft, the origins of various terms, the legitimacy of various aspects of different traditions. We are concerned with our present and our future.

13. We do not accept the concept of absolute evil nor do we worship any entity known as "Satan" or "the Devil" as defined by the Christian tradition. We do not seek power through the suffering of others nor accept that personal benefit can be derived only by denial to another.

14. We believe that we should seek within Nature that which is contributory to our health and well–being.

Photo © 1993 Malcolm Brenner / Eyes Open

Rites of Passage

by Chas S. Clifton

The Craft had been pretty much an adult activity for me until one night in 1977. Our coven used to meet in a former school building on the High Plains of eastern Colorado. The building's furnace was inoperative, so we had installed a wood stove in the one classroom that served as the sanctuary. On winter nights, warmed by our ritual baths, we would robe, slip on shoes or boots, and dash across from the high priest and priestess's living quarters across a gravel driveway to the former school building. There the tile floors, blond brick walls, and aluminum window frames mixed incongruously with the trappings of Pagandom. Imagine a schoolroom in Anyplace, U.S.A., redone with hangings, altar, candles, and Pagan art: that pretty well describes the scene.

There was less need to rush on summer nights. Crickets chirped, the day's heat abated, a distant oil well pump engine muttered, moths circled the outdoor lights. On one such night in July a young woman named Sher carried her baby son Josh around the circle for the coven's blessing—a "Wiccaning," as the ceremony has became known. Perhaps that was the first time I heard the word "Wiccaning." It was definitely the first time I had seen anyone that young in the ritual circle: the promise of another Pagan generation.

Looking back, I do not know what has become of Sher and Josh. The school building in Morgan County passed into other hands a year or two later. The semi-communal life that had centered on it dissipated for the usual set of reasons that are the bane of most such experiments. There was too little money, too few firm rules, ambivalent leaders, too little practical vision. And so, despite a few shining moments,[1] that rural experiment dwindled and ended like countless others. But while it existed, it provided a glimpse of a larger Pagandom. Borrowing a term from Indian people, we sometimes referred to it as "the rez" (i.e., the reservation). Despite the poverty, junked pickup trucks, and all the rest, it offered a psychic refuge. The dominant culture stopped at the turn-off from the county road; here a different culture existed.

This book is about the ritual glue that binds a Pagan culture. In contrast, much writing on modern Paganism, whether Witchcraft or some other form (see below for a lengthier discussion of these terms), seems to assume that the reader is a young, single adult. Perhaps that is the image of the "seeker," the way the Fool is shown in some of the more esoterically inclined Tarot decks. At most, the reader is seen as a member of a coven or other group made up of adults. This collection of writings, however, tries to take a longer view with the long-term goal of producing a living Pagan culture.

If modern Pagan traditions are to persist and even to have any effect on the world community in an overt way, they must encompass people of all ages, not only young adults. *Rites of Passage*, therefore, is organized according to some of life's significant markers: birth, puberty, adulthood, partnership, maturity or eldership, and finally death. None of these occur in a social vacuum, but always in relation to other people.

But as Pagans (particularly if we are parents) we face a special set of social issues. We live in a society whose views of how the cosmos is constructed often vary dramatically from ours. At the same time, we must participate in it; we cannot pretend that we do not. Consequently, we find ourselves always taking positions on a continuum between *separation*—or tension—and *continuity*. First, we cannot but feel somewhat separate from the so-called Judeo-Christian culture whose assumptions, as Karen Charboneau-Harrison outlines in her chapter, "Raising a Pagan Child," are so often alien to ours. Yet we cannot put up psychological walls and create our own ghetto—that way lies stagnation. Our way is not to remove ourselves and try to live a "pure" life unpolluted by contact with "unbelievers."

Besides, we share the dominant culture's political institutions. We usually send our children to its schools. We breathe the same air, drink the same water, and produce as much sewage as anyone else. We do not exist in isolation from the larger world; indeed, such delusions of isolation are something Paganism tries to overcome. And, of course, we have always taken pleasure in recovering the Pagan elements in such holidays as Christmas and Easter. Not only does that make for effective celebrations, but it means we need not feel left out during the late December festivities, for example.

On the other hand, Wicca and other types of modern Paganism do not represent a reform movement or an esoteric flowering of the dominant religious faiths. This root difference creates tension between us and the dominant culture. Wicca presents a radical critique of the dominant forms of spirituality more than it seeks accommodation with them. The chief accommodation it does seek is simply the equality under civil law provided by the United States Constitution or any other nation's guarantee of religious liberty (those that enforce them!).

Wicca does not even adopt the vaguely Protestant cultural camouflage of such bodies as Unitarianism, Mormonism, Christian Science, or other traditions that have kept more or less mainstream forms of architecture, worship, reverence for "scripture," political organization, and behavior while deviating considerably in doctrine from mainstream Christianity.[2] Nor have we attempted to take Christian doctrines and "esotericize" them in the style of some "metaphysical Christians" who, for example, might treat the 12 apostles as "12 rays." Wicca does none of these. We have no need for dedicated worship buildings; we can meet and function anywhere—often preferring to be outdoors, conditions permitting. We certainly have no capital-S Scripture, and I hope we never do.[3] Our worship may vary from mass celebrations to small-group focused magical workings, but they never involve a passive congregation being harangued from a pulpit. Only in political organization do Wiccan bodies sometimes resemble other denominations, and that similarity occurs just because we operate under the same federal, state, and local laws as anyone else.[4]

And most obvious of all, we describe ourselves by terms like "Witch," a word that was once a death sentence, or more mildly as "Pagan," which in my the-saurus falls into some shadow category between "ani-mist" and "atheist," even while carrying with it an echo of flickering firelight and clinking tambourines. These terms are enough to create a degree of separation from the dominant culture unlikely to be completely bridged in the near future.

A digression: Contributors to the *Witchcraft Today* series tend to drift back and forth between "Paganism" and "Witchcraft" or "Wicca" or "Craft," and between "Witch" and "Pagan" (both capitalized as proper nouns denoting adherents of this religious movement). I find general agreement that Paganism is the more inclusive word while Witchcraft is one of its components or sub-sets. One widely read Pagan writer, Otter Zell, describes traditional Witchcraft as "European shamanism, origi-nally in the context of a Pagan culture," and he also sees indigenous Pagan traditions around the globe as shar-ing such elements as acknowledging Mother Earth, having seasonal celebrations, and utilizing the ritual circle and the four cosmic directions, Mystery initia-tions, rites of passage, divination and so on.[5]

Another Pagan editor characterizes Paganism as "worship, spontaneous ritual, celebration, and bril-liantly colored ribbons. . . . worship, celebration, myths," in comparison to Witchcraft, which she described as containing such elements as "exercises in ESP, spellcraft, and a core set of rituals designed to be used repeatedly because the repetition of the pattern is what gains the power. . . . herbs, astrology, spells, astral projection, and [giving its practitioners] control over their lives."[6]

In many cultures only certain people are drawn to becoming religious specialists, and Pagan culture appears to be following the same path. I see no problem with this but rather view it as inevitable. End of digression.

Today's Witches and other Pagans can claim even more forms of cultural continuity, more significant ones than corn dollies and Morris dancing. In the United States, at least, we can claim equal rights to the Enlightenment heritage of "natural rights" that Thomas Jefferson summarized as "life, liberty, and the pursuit of happiness." We are fortunate that our nation was constituted at a point in history when at least some political leaders believed that such rights, including freedom of religion, were inherent in human beings and not granted by any outside authority. Consider that in the late 1600s, only a century before this republic's founding, New England suffered the Salem witch trials. In addition, Quakers, Baptists, and other dissenters were hung, flogged, or banished from that "city upon a hill," that "New Jerusalem" called the Massachusetts Bay Colony. Meanwhile, in colonial Virginia the pre-revolutionary Anglican clergy constantly agitated against the presence of other Protestant ministers although they did not so often resort to violence against dissenters. We are fortunate that the colonists of the late 1700s had learned to be somewhat more tolerant than their predecessors.

Therefore, despite the contradictions of this nation's beginnings—the praise of natural rights versus the official acceptance of slavery being the greatest—we can be glad that many of the nation's founders began to identify themselves with their new land, and in the words of the Virginia patriot Richard Henry Lee, "wondered out loud, 'why we should not lay our rights upon the broadest bottom, the ground of nature.'"[7]

In fact, the writings of those times are still worth studying in the face of Christian Reconstruction and other movements designed to return the United States not, in fact, to any purer time of its existence, but actually to the intolerance of the earlier Massachusetts Bay Colony. Ironically, those who exercise their natural rights to chose their own religious views and to be protected in them by the Constitution are closer to the founders' original intent than the bigots arguing that America was founded to be a "Christian nation."[8]

But not all of the original Massachusetts settlers were Puritans, and this often-forgotten fact introduces another point at which modern Pagans can claim continuity with a larger tradition—nature religion. One of our favorite colonial figures ought to be Thomas Morton, who erected the first Maypole at his settlement in 1627 and held "the first interracial [whites and Indians] Neo-Pagan gathering in North America," dedicated to Aphrodite herself.[9] (At least one modern Pagan lineage is indeed named after Morton.) Chased back to England by Puritan authorities, Morton stirred up more trouble in Maine before his death in 1647.

The Maypole was reincarnated in the 1770s as the Liberty Tree, meeting place for the Sons of Liberty and frequent emblem on revolutionary flags. Historians of religion see in it the traditional *axis mundi*—Yggdrasil and all the other trees that connected the Underworld, Middle Earth, and the Upper World.[10] Expressing the eternal cycle of death and rebirth in measured 18th-century prose, Thomas Jefferson wrote of it that "The tree of liberty must be refreshed from time to time with the blood of patriots and tyrants. It is its natural manure."[11]

Again, I will not deny that the reality of early America did not always live up to the image. Too many people looked upon the land not for religious inspiration but just as raw material to be chewed up.

We all know this goes on today: the tension between "harmony" and "mastery" is another story. But we as Pagans can claim continuity with a solid North American tradition of turning to Nature as a source of sacred values equal to or better than those derived from someone's Holy Book. This tradition includes not just the big names like Henry Thoreau, John Muir, or Aldo Leopold, but countless others who were willing to let This Place speak to them. People may claim to own land, but no one owns Nature. Pagans have a religious vocabulary for the interconnectedness of all life, a concept non-Pagans must reach intellectually. Whether this vocabulary will somehow save us from ecological catastrophe is yet to be seen, but it gives us a starting point.

Rites of Passage and the Pagan Community

Although Paganism offers no supreme authority figures to whom we turn in defiance of larger society, as long as we are a religious minority, the community is in a sense our larger "family." As we attune ourselves on a yearly cycle, so we mark passages and transitions in our lives. This volume in the *Witchcraft Today* series is organized chronologically as the contributors seek to describe actual Pagan rites of passage, not just how they should be done but how they *are* being done.

The term "rites of passage" became popular after a book by that name was written by the anthropologist Arnold van Gennep (1873–1957).[12] Too often, however, we confuse "rites of passage" with initiations and with puberty rites in particular, and we focus on their individual elements to the detriment of the communal element. For example, beginning in the late 1970s a "vision-quest" industry arose based loosely on the practices of some Plains Indian tribes. For a sum of money, a man or woman may go with a small group to some place of dramatic scenery like the Utah canyonlands for what amounts to a camping trip with a solo component. (Many people in the vision-quest business consider themselves to be "outdoor educators" with their roots in Outward Bound and similar programs.) But when we look at their experience in terms of Van Gennep's now classic three-part formula, we see *separation*, yes, and *transition*, but then comes *incorporation* ... into what? Ultimately, the vision quester is a customer, so she or he is incorporated only into the group of former customers. Society—thus far—pays no attention.

Looking at men's experience only, Ray Raphael's book *The Men from the Boys*[13] contains many interviews with men who in effect designed their own "initiations." Their experience included difficult physical jobs, military service with or without combat, rock climbing, sexual experiences, and more. He even interviewed one "Radical Faerie" Witch. "Somehow," he writes, "the results of these freestyle and piecemeal initiations are rarely as convincing as the single, all-encompassing initiation into a more homogeneous culture."[14]

When we consider initiations in tribal culture, whether of young women or young men, we notice that usually no one fails. A low-tech tribal culture cannot afford too much Social Darwinism—survival of the fittest, elimination of the weak. Life itself will eliminate the weak, and it is in the tribe's best interest to have as many functioning, mature men and women as possible. Tribal initiations are not a matter of "win or die, sink or swim." Instead, they educate the initiates, develop their inner strength, give them a taste of life's sacred dimension, and return them to the community.

"Which community?" is the modern response. I have too often seen Pagandom turned into an exclusive club, like a college fraternity, and I grit my teeth when Pagans start chattering about "cowans" or "mundanes." Turning Pagandom into an exclusive club means going too far down the tension/continuity axis towards "tension," and as I mentioned above, we are already far enough in that direction. One becomes a Witch for many reasons, but a desire to shock other people is not an adequate reason. Our puberty rites must not only reincorporate the initiate into the growing Pagan community, but somehow into a larger community that we are also part of. Perhaps as part of the Pagan adulthood rite the priest or priestess should accompany the initiates to the county courthouse where they then register to vote—although that would automatically set the date for initiation at age 18 in the United States. At least that would make use of one societally recognized marker, low-key as it is.

In traditional societies, Arnold van Gennep noted, puberty rites rarely coincided with physiological puberty, which is something we often forget. Girls' first menstruation occurs at a variety of ages, and boys lack even that clear marker. For example, in those cultures that practice it, male circumcision is performed at any time from shortly after birth to age 12, 13, or even older, depending on the locale. Instead, these societies usually used some system of age groups: a group of boys from about ages 12 to 15 might all make the transition from "children" to "bachelors" at once, depending on the circumstances.

About This Book

"Rites of passage" can begin before birth, but more often babies are themselves welcomed into the community; the term "Wiccaning" was devised to refer to such a ceremony, and Trish Telesco provides a sample approach.

Thus far relatively few children have grown up in modern Pagan households: Karen Charboneau-Harrison offers her own experience as child and as mother while Anodea Judith interviews a group of young adults who grew up in the thick of West Coast Pagandom.

The majority of modern Pagans, however, find the movement as teenagers or young adults. Judy Harrow's "Other People's Kids" offers a way to meet the needs of would-be Pagans who are still legal minors, while a Boston-area Witch, Darcie, whose academic training was in anthropology, re-examines the experience of "conversion," or as most Pagans would describe it, "coming home."

Our larger society does not mark the transition from youth to adulthood in any clear way: that was the point of Ray Raphael's book from men's point of view, but of course it is true for women also. Oz, a Wiccan priestess in Albuquerque, works with adult women who feel they missed that step in their lives; from a magickal point of view, rewriting the past is sometimes feasible. For many young men and some women, military service is often held out as the "marker" for adulthood; in her chapter, "Initiation by Ordeal," Judy Harrow looks at the experiences of Pagan military veterans.

Marriage also is frequently considered a passage into adulthood, but Wicca in particular uses two types of socially recognized bondings: unions that are considered permanent and those that are made for a specific length of time. Jeff Charboneau-Harrison offers some thoughts and ritual ideas for "handfasting," as Pagan marriages are usually called, combined with a deeper look at the psychic dynamics of marriage.

Dealing with later life, Grey Cat, a Tennessee priestess and former editor of a newsletter called *The Crone Papers*, considers just what it is that makes a Wiccan "elder." And since everyone's life contains some grief, Paul Suliin has written on coping with it from a Pagan perspective.

Finally, Oz uses the culture-clashing funeral rites of Pagan poet and songwriter Gwydion Pendderwen, who died in 1982, to open both the magickal and mundane issues surrounding death within the Pagan community.

After all, rites of passage are more than just "social glue." As Tom Driver, another modern writer on ritual, states, the "gifts of ritual are order, community, and transformation."[15] We do not perform these rituals just as social exercises but with the intent of effecting some subtle change—hence "working" as an alternate term for magickal operations. Driver describes transformation as "not simply a transformation of subjectivity, leaving the external world unchanged except perhaps in appearance," but "in short, a reordering of totality."[16]

To this end, most contributors have included suggestions for actual rites of passage upon which experienced practitioners may build. Wicca makes no distinction between "religion" and "magic," let alone taking the deracinated stance of so many modern observers: that "magic" is degenerate religion or "false science." Instead, we as Pagans should enter these rites sincerely, opening them to include not just people, but spirits, animals, and ancestors. (Great-grandmother may have been a fundamentalist in this life, but she is probably more open-minded in the Otherworld.) So let us not just build community but strive for genuine transformation.

NOTES

[1]See, for example, the fish-catching episode described in chapter 13 of Margot Adler's *Drawing Down the Moon* (Boston: Beacon Press, 1986).

[2]All the traditions named chiefly developed in the 19th century, of course, when the cultural power of the American Protestant hegemony was at its height. There simply were no other models in their founders' minds to follow. The Unitarian church, however, now has a flourishing Pagan wing.

[3]The investigations of the Gardnerian "Book of Shadows" carried out in the 1980s by Doreen Valiente, Aidan Kelly, and others should have been enough to thoroughly disprove claims made of its pre-20th-century origins.

[4]For more discussion of Witchcraft's legal concerns, see Pete Pathfinder, "Witchcraft and the Law," in Chas S. Clifton, ed. *Witchcraft Today Book One: The Modern Craft Movement* (St. Paul: Llewellyn Publications, 1992).

[5]Otter Zell, Editorial response in "Green Egg Forum," *Green Egg* 97 (Summer 1992), 56.

[6]Morven, Editorial response in letters column, *Harvest* 12:4 (Spring Equinox 1992), 12.

[7]Catherine L. Albanese, *Nature Religion in America*, (Chicago: University of Chicago Press, 1990), 54.

[8]From a magickal standpoint, study of these documents and the writings of the Founders is one way for American Pagans to contact the best parts of the nation's group soul.

[9]Peter Lamborn Wilson, "Caliban's Masque: Spiritual Anarchy and the Wild Man in Colonial America," *Gnosis* 23 (Spring 1992), 56-63.

[10]Albanese, 52-3.

[11]Thomas Jefferson, Letter to W. S. Smith, 13 November 1787.

[12]Arnold van Gennep, *The Rites of Passage* (Chicago: University of Chicago Press, 1960).

[13]Ray Raphael, *The Men from the Boys: Rites of Passage in Male America* (Lincoln: University of Nebraska Press, 1988).

[14]Raphael, 192.

[15]Tom F. Driver, *The Magic of Ritual* (San Francisco: HarperSan Francisco, 1991), 132.

[16]Driver, 176.

ABOUT THE AUTHOR

Active in the Craft since the mid-1970s, Chas S. Clifton lives in southern Colorado, where he divides his time between freelance writing and photography, teaching college writing, and contract wildlife research. He has published numerous articles in magazines ranging from *Fate* to *Western Outdoors* and serves as contributing editor of *Gnosis: A Journal of the Western Inner Traditions*. He is also the author of *The Encyclopedia of Heresies and Heretics* (ABC-Clio, 1992).

Photo © 1993 Malcolm Brenner / Eyes Open

Having a Magickal Child:
Childbirth and Wiccaning

by Trish Telesco

Many Pagans are seeking ways to make the entire experience of childbirth from conception to naming more warm, welcoming, and magickal. I cannot imagine a more exquisite way for a soul to grow and eventually become part of the Wiccan/Pagan family than to be surrounded by spiritual energy in this way.

Having a child is a unique transition, a passage from singularity into bearing life and being responsible for that little spirit's development along a path of beauty. This transition presents an immense opportunity for all involved to discover a new fullness, a remarkable dimension in their relationships. These changes are not without struggle, yet the struggle is worthwhile as long as the extension of love is your goal.

For additional insight and information in writing this article, I turned to two friends, David and Kym, who were able to bring a beautiful baby girl named Chelsea into the world in their own home. Chelsea's conception, carriage, and birth exemplified the extra spiritual dimension I hope to convey in this article. To David and Kym's experience I have added a little of my own experience, plus knowledge shared by a wide variety of people over the years. My thanks to David and Kym for helping with this effort so that many families can be likewise enriched.

The Birth Partner's Role

The role of a mother's birth partner, whether life mate, friend, or family member, should not be overlooked nor underestimated. The emotional and physical support the partner can give will be invaluable. Whoever the chosen partner is, you should trust him or her with not only your well-being but that of your child. Discuss how you would like your partner to participate on all levels of the birth experience—physical, emotional, and spiritual. From the first day you know you want a child until well after delivery, this individual will act in many capacities, including mentor, assistant, organizer, and confidant, so consider your choices well.

What role your partner takes in your child's life during birth and in later years may depend on your situation. For example, if you are married or handfasted, your partner will often be your life mate. On the other hand, if you are the wife or lover of a squeamish man, you might need to have a partner to act in the position of birthing coach. If you are a single mother, this individual will not only be a birthing coach, but might later be given charge over your child in the role of godparent, sponsor, or guide for many spiritual transitions of their own. Keep both the present and future in mind as you work with this partner to create your magickal child. Finally, should you be planning to conceive by artificial insemination, you may wish to find a partner who can symbolically enact the conception ritual with you, knowing that in magick symbols can become what they represent.

No matter your personal scenario, birth partners should be well-respected parts of the entire birth process. Confide in them, love them, and allow them to share their love and support with you.

Conception

Remember before choosing to become pregnant that childbirth is a lifetime commitment. Children are one of the most challenging and educational experiences of any life or relationship, requiring patience, understanding, and heaping amounts of love. Whenever anyone comes to me with questions on conception, the first thing I ask is if they have thought through all the financial, physical, and emotional changes that a baby will bring. If so, then we can go on to the next step. There are enough abandoned and abused children in this world already. As magickal people we have a responsibility to build a life for ourselves and our young filled with quality living. This cannot happen if we are ill-prepared for all the wonders and trials children can bring.

Interestingly enough, fertility advice has been one of the age-old functions of wise woman. In years gone by, they would take a young woman by the hand and gently share with her simple methods to help the body prepare for pregnancy, often calming many fears in the process. Some of this oral tradition has been safely guarded by mothers and elders over the years and fortunately is slowly filtering into the magickal community again.

Much of the advice regarding the entire birth process is basically more practical than magickal. Words of wisdom to relax, eat right, get plenty of rest, exercise, and just generally let nature take her course appear frequently in conversations with those who are versed in the subject. Even modern medicine gives us the same guidance. Thus our second step (with or without magickal aid) is to be sure we are physically and emotionally prepared to have a child. Don't leave your common sense behind on this journey.

The next important thing to remember is that even though you are trying to conceive, pregnancy alone is not the goal of your lovemaking. This is a mistake many couples fall into. They focus so much on conception that they become tense even to the point of being unable to perform. While timing has a certain role in instances where conception is difficult, if you start initiating or abstaining from sex based solely on that guideline, you will probably not succeed in your goal. Emotional factors are important. The lovemaking which creates a child needs to be as sensual and memorable as the baby itself! Don't be afraid to be creative and tender. Bless your room and prepare a sacred space, but within that boundary, two people playing and loving in unity is the most important thing.

Both partners (those involved in actually physically producing a child) should try to eliminate as many toxins as possible from their diets, including drugs, alcohol, cigarettes, and meat that is not organically produced. Some studies also suggest care in your exposure to television, waterbeds, electric blankets, or any large appliance which could disrupt your natural biomagnetic energy flow. In addition, wearing loose underclothing helps decrease micro-organisms which are detrimental to productivity and keeps the sperm cooler after sex, thus allowing it to live longer. Again, on the surface these ideas seem very mundane, but much of our magickal wisdom comes from good old country observation!

If you find you are having difficulty conceiving, remember that taking your temperature, douching with warm vinegar and water, gaining a few pounds, stopping the use of tampons, using egg whites as a lubricant, and maintaining your sense of humor can also aid the fertility process. Herbalists often additionally recommend vitamin C, vitamins B-6 and B-12, calcium, zinc, ginseng, black cohosh, sarsaparilla root, and vitamin E be included in your diet.

Below you will find a recipe for a natural herb tea to drink for several weeks before you plan to have a conception ritual. In preparing this tea, visualize yourself like a budding tree or egg ready to burst (egg visualizations are common parts of fertility rites). Ask the God/dess of your choice (see list on pages 35–36) to direct her or his productive energy into the herbs and thus into your body. Visualize this each time you prepare and drink the tea.

Fertility Tea

1 tsp. red clover flower	1 tsp. red raspberry leaf
1 tsp. blessed thistle	1 tsp. alfalfa
1 tsp. chamomile	1 tsp. dandelion
1 tsp. sarsaparilla root	1 tsp. licorice root

Warm these herbs in a stoneware container filled with 2–3 cups of water for about 30 minutes until the herbs are well infused. Place them in a larger container, adding water, and keep this in a sunny place for 24 hours. Strain and drink a cup a day until your ritual. To this tea, you may also add a visualization of taking in the sperm and its growing within you, even as the tea is warming your stomach.

Besides these attempts to improve the fertility and preparedness of both partners, magickal mandalas which incorporate the visual image of an egg or concentric circles which artistically parody the incoming sperm are very helpful to conception. How you create these images and carry them with you is a very personal matter, but above all else listen to your inner voice. Choose symbols which are deeply private and meaningful and keep them near your heart, or if possible your womb, at all times. Your partner may also carry one near his private parts or heart to increase the potency of your efforts.

Other fertility magick includes offering an egg by planting it deep in rich soil with a flowering seed above it (just as you hope your seed will flower), charging a crystal egg with productive energy and carrying it at all times (this can be given to the child later as a protective amulet), or even a necklace of seeds—all of which should be meaningful to you—that again can be used by the child in a magickal circle later in life.[1]

Conception Rituals: With incense, soft music, timing, and creativity, a conception ritual can also be one of the most beautiful forms of loving known. Within the boundaries of sacred space, where time and limits have little meaning, amazing things can be born, not the least of which is a child. Here, you and your partner can become likened to the God and Goddess whose energy of love gave birth to the universe.

The date chosen for your ritual should correspond to the woman's fertile period if possible. If possible, the date should be one that is special to the two of you as individuals. The room selected needs to be private and filled with happy memories. Most couples choose to make a child's image for the altar, often filling the room with rose petals for love, musk and vervain for fertility, basil for harmony of purpose, vanilla for vitality, and cinnamon for luck (serendipity never hurts).

If possible the couple should spend time alone and together in meditation before lovemaking begins so that the goal of their evening is firmly fixed in their minds. A prayer to your patron God or Goddess and a small whisper of welcome to a waiting soul is also appropriate. Instead of a ritual cup full of wine, consider milk, a more maternal liquid.

Yellow, being a creative color, is good to adorn the space either in sheets, candles or an altar cloth and sprigs of yarrow, parsley, and St. John's wort gathered on Midsummer's Eve should be hung over the bed (these have long been considered potent fertility aids). If these herbs are not readily available, I suggest the image of a stork as an appropriate substitute. It may seem silly, but the long association between this bird and the coming of a child can have similar effects on our subconscious, thereby giving our magick a little boost.

If you have chosen artificial insemination as a means of conception, this half of the ritual is done the night or morning before the procedure, with the rest following when you are home and rested. Alternatively, if you have decided on adoption, you might want to perform this part of the rite just before you put in your applications so that the God/dess can help direct the right child to your home.[2]

Once you are finished with the ritual, keep the image of the child (a cloth doll filled with herbs is good) near you. Care for it and talk to it. Leave it on your altar or in safekeeping when you are away from home. If no pregnancy occurs, try again. Do not allow this to discourage you. You have not "failed"—there are a large variety of factors which could hinder your reproductive process, not the least of which is simply it not being the "right time." The God/dess knows your desire and will find a way to answer those hopes in one way or another.

Pregnancy

Once a child has been conceived, the tasks of physical and spiritual maintenance do not stop. If anything they become more important to the well-being of both the baby and its parent(s). It is never too soon to start thinking about your baby in terms of a little person. This means talking and playing music to it as well as creating small items which can represent the child in your personal magickal work in the home. By so doing, you allow the baby to be an active participant in the spiritual health of the entire household even before birth. Appropriate items for spell components or decoration for the altar might include a bottle, rattle, pacifier, stuffed toy or any other little gift which you plan to give the baby upon arrival in this world.[3]

It is nice to mark the time during your pregnancy in some personally significant manner. Some people make a blanket or other handcrafted item which can also be later given to their baby for protection. My husband, for example, cross-stitched a four-color, equal-armed ("Celtic") cross that was later placed in my son's crib as a good-health token. If you do want to make something, it is good to work during the waxing to full

Moon so that your child may grow as strong and beautiful as the item you create. Many such items when crafted with loving care eventually become special magickal tools for the child later in life, especially at occasions such as puberty, handfasting, or the birth of another generation.

Another means of observing the time is to have a small ritual of thanksgiving at the end of each month or each trimester, the last trimester's celebration corresponding with the birth itself. In this instance, the first commemoration should be a private thanksgiving to note your passage from Maiden to Mother aspect by way of leaving a small offering (milk or grain are perfectly acceptable) to the God/dess for your health and blessings.[4] The second observance might be done with friends as an accent to a baby shower. This is a good time to welcome the soul/spirit of your child into the circle of your family and friends. Finally the third ritual would be performed after the mother and child return home.

During this time it is good to walk and swim, unless your doctor advises you not to. Continue visualizing the child growing strong and healthy in your womb (always head-down to help decrease the chance of breech birth). Realize this small being is already a part of your home and heart. Consult books about pregnancy and children (see suggested reading at the end of the article) and try to assimilate the changes in your body. (Those around you will have some adjustments to make too!) There are some excellent publications which can help you prepare for these changes and meet them healthily. The information in these types of texts will assist with everything from nausea and fatigue to yeast infections.

Birth

During the last trimester and frequently even sooner, people begin to think about how they want their child brought into this world. Thankfully, there are now alternatives to the impersonal drabness of many hospital rooms. Many modernized facilities offer birthing rooms which are cheerfully decorated and where family members are allowed to participate in the birth process.

If you are interested in having a birthing room, you should let your doctor know when you go into labor to see if one can be arranged. Otherwise, most hospitals will allow you to take a few personal items into the labor rooms to make it more personable. The creative contemporary magician can, of course, make sure these objects are blessed and charged with positive energy for the occasion beforehand.

If you are going to have your child in the hospital, another question to consider is whether or not you plan to have "natural" childbirth, and it is a decision which should be made by both partners. Most magickal people opt for this approach due to concern over the effect of various painkillers on the fetus and a desire to fully experience the birth with total awareness. I agree that this is probably the best approach, especially if you are able to have the baby at home or to magickally prepare your birthing space at the hospital. However, if labor becomes too difficult to bear, remember that medical science can help you. It is very important that you listen to the signals your body is giving you along with your inner voice.

Obviously your magickal alternatives at the hospital are not as varied, but you can quietly envision your sacred space and call on the aid of your God/desses. You can carry small magickal items with you to wear or keep nearby, have your gifts ready for the child, and continue simple versions of focused visualizations—which are usually recommended for natural birth anyway!

Also, don't forget to talk to your doctor, knowing that his/her attitude will often reflect that of the hospital. If the doctor is inflexible, I suggest asking for alternative medical references from other Wiccan/Pagan friends. Pregnancy is not a disease which needs to be expelled from the body, nor should it be treated that way. Once the right doctor is found, you can then share your desires. For example, if both you and your child are healthy at the delivery, there is no reason why some of your personal religious preferences shouldn't be observed at the time of birth, such as giving the child a braid of your hair to wear on its ankle as a special connection between the two of you, or not spanking the child on birth but allowing you to nurse.

Home Birth and Midwives: Another birthing choice gaining popularity, especially among Pagans, is that of home births with trained midwives. While this is not recommended for people with physical problems (heart conditions and diabetes, for example) or in instances where the pregnancy has been difficult or has shown signs of a distressed fetus, it can be a marvelous experience in the case of a normal, healthy pregnancy to term. To find a good midwife, you can contact the Midwives Alliance of North America, P.O. Box 5337, Cheyenne, Wyoming 82003—telephone (307) 637-5737. This group will be able to share with you the history of midwifery and essential hints on finding someone you feel confident about. Another address to try is The American College of Nurse-Midwives, 1522 K Street NW, Suite 1120, Washington D.C. 20005—telephone (202) 347-5445.

If you are having your child at home, you should
try to find a class which addresses the concerns of
birthing in this atmosphere. A group called Informed
Homebirth and Parenting, founded in 1977, offers sem-
inars in various locations. More information on this
group is available in the book *Special Delivery* (see reading list below), or you may write to Informed Homebirth, P.O. Box 3675, Ann Arbor, Michigan 48106 or call
(313) 662-6857. Most people feel much better equipped
if they have trained people to ask questions of and
share the experience with.

At home you have the option of choosing attendants, each of whom should have some type of chore to
perform during labor. One might chant softly to help
concentration, another keep an eye on music or incense,
and another get water. The mother should be bathed in
warm water and herbs to relax her, and candles lit to
soften the atmosphere. Songs to the God/dess may be
sung, and gentle prayers lifted for the safe delivery of
the young one.

At this point, before labor becomes difficult, gifts
may be given which can be symbolic or useful. The best
items are those which signify endurance and laughter,
both of which will be needed in the hours ahead. This
may very well be the original version of a shower!

The birthing space should be tidy and friendly.
Visualizations of water moving downward are extremely
potent after the water has already broken. All in attendance should be smudged, and someone should have
marked the sacred space according to the parent(s)'
wishes.[5] This is a hallowed ground where a new soul is
about to join you. Greet it with joy, respect, and love.

In some ancient cultures it was traditional to have
a linen cloth prepared by painting a special verse or

name of a favored family God or Goddess on it. This cloth was then steeped in protective, calming herbs and laid across the womb to insure safe childbirth. Chamomile makes an excellent choice for this in that it is perfectly safe, and naturally calming in its scent. Again this chore can be done by someone in attendance, perhaps even another child to help them feel more a part of the experience.

Kym told me that during her labor time ceased to exist. There was only the birth-time when all boundaries were flung aside. As she moved with her contractions she spoke the words "solid as a rock, safe within the harbor, ancient as a stone and strong as the sea. Solid as a rock, set deep within the mother and water that flows round me", while someone else in the room chanted "born of water, cleansing, power, healing, changing ... we are." Ginger-root compresses were used to help ease the pain of passage, and everyone around her gave gentle touches of reassurance.

Finally when the child is born, as was the case with Chelsea, it is washed in warm water and placed on the mother's belly to nurse, giving the immediate bonding so important to emotionally healthy children. Those in attendance join hands and sing or chant or laugh in thankfulness for the miracle before them. Hugs are exchanged and later an offering of flower petals is released to the winds so that others might be similarly blessed.

Wiccaning: Dedication and Naming

The amount of time you wait after birth to dedicate, bless, or name your child is a personal decision. Many ancient cultures waited anywhere from three days to three months to be certain the child lived. Since we are blessed to have medical science decreasing the likelihood of infant mortality, you should choose a moment which has special significance to you (Some people choose a year and a day after the conception, for example). I also suggest you remember this date, as it could be commemorated with a passage rite when the child becomes an adult member of the family.

The welcome and naming ritual should be filled with items and words that are comfortable on your lips and that reflect your feelings. The altar can be decorated with fresh flowers for new beginnings, white candles representing the purity and precious nature of life, a container of milk, salt, incense, and soil. This way, by touching each to the child's third eye, you can bless him or her with all elements and charge his or her life with the protection of all guardians.

Everything in the room including the gifts should be well thought out. Most children enjoy lively colors, happy sounds, and clean smells. This is a joyous occasion where you introduce your new magickal being to the world of friends and loved ones. These people need roles in this ritual too, for their lives will influence the child in the years ahead. It is also their responsibility to answer the call to tend a new soul even as you are now.

Words need not be fancy. In fact, one of the most beautiful ritual dedications ever done was depicted in Alex Halley's novel *Roots*. Holding the child to the sky and saying, "Behold the only thing greater than yourself" is a very empowering action. It tells this young one of all that he or she can be, and the wonders of the universe she or he has just entered. If you continue to foster this attitude, you cannot help but have a very beautiful child who naturally lives in reciprocity with Mother Earth.

A Child's Passing

Although they are not pleasant to think about, miscarriage, stillbirth, abortion, and sudden infant death ("crib death") must also be considered. No matter the circumstances, each of these situations means emotional turmoil for the mother and those who love her.

I cannot be judgmental about abortion. It is a personal decision and one that comes after no small amount of consideration. I myself have never miscarried nor had a child die, but after worrying at the hospital for a week when my son was born with underdeveloped lungs, I can begin to touch the feelings of those who undergo these losses.

No matter at what stage you believe a soul is brought into the human body, when a child is conceived a soul waits specifically for that lovingly created shell. So perhaps the best way to handle any of these situations is as you would handle the passing of anyone that you cared about. At a minimum, I would suggest a private meditation with only a few trusted friends or family members to give support.

As you settle yourself into a contemplative state, breathing deeply, you mentally take yourself to some place that is warm and welcoming—a place where you always felt safe and happy. Next, verbally welcome the child's spirit. Do not have any expectations as to how it will appear or communicate, but simply let it know that it is well-received in this sacred space.

Next, share your feelings with the child's spirit. Do not hold back: be totally honest—and honest with yourself. If you opted for an abortion, share the reasons why and then send the soul on its way, wishing it a better life with someone prepared and desiring a child. If you miscarried, share your grief, your sense of loss, and your hopes for the future. This is an emotional experience, which is why your family and friends are here. Lean on them and allow your sorrows, confusion, remorse, and regrets be washed away by your tears. Crying is one of the greatest cleansing experiences known to the human spirit.

When you are finished, release the spirit, thanking it kindly for choosing you and wishing it blessings on its journey. Likewise, speak a prayer to your God/dess for your own blessing and happiness in the future.

This ritual is not meant to be an instant fix for all the wounds you feel; however, it will help. It is but one step on the road, a road that may or may not include children. Either way, you have made an attempt to gain inner peace, perhaps the most important step to take toward your own heart too.

Adoption

Since natural birth is not an option for everyone, we must also consider adoption's place in rituals of birth and Wiccaning. While adopting a child can be an even greater challenge than giving birth, adoption offers the knowledge that this young one is a true gift, something nature could not provide or something the adoptive parents have decided to do for the welfare of another being. This decision should be celebrated with as much joy as if the child had been had been born of the mother's own womb.

If you have adopted a child due to physical limitations, this action probably marks the end of a very long, emotionally difficult period for you and your partner. If you are adopting simply to open your home to one in need, this too is a beautiful gesture. In both cases, we need to approach the moment the child enters the home in a way similar to that in which we approach the passage out of the womb. To them, this truly is a strange, new world they are entering.

Obviously the types of rites you perform will depend greatly on the age of the child. Babies can go through similar rites to those of naming given above. Older children, however, present a different set of variables. I suggest some kind of welcoming party for them where each person in the household or family gives the child an item which signifies their hopes for the future. For example, homemade bread can be shared so that your new family member will never want or a cup given so that their life is always full of hospitality. Toys appropriate to the age group are also a good idea, as they help give the child a greater sense of security and permanence.

Bringing Up Baby

Do not stop your physical or spiritual care of self and child once all the commotion of birth and naming are over. This has only been the first step of a long journey in which you will learn as much as your child! Now you must begin to consider how to best raise this spirit in the magickal home and unique atmosphere which you have created from the beginning of your desire for a baby.

While some do not agree, I think there is nothing wrong with sharing simple magicks with children. Half the time they understand and use them far better than we do because of their simple acceptance of the unseen world and total trust. It is this lovely vision in children, and their capacity to bring magick to life, which should be fostered in early years, not dogma or rhetoric.

This is not to say that all children of a magickal home will adopt Wicca as their faith, just as not all Christian homes have Christian children. However, teaching them to respect the earth, enjoy its bountiful beauty, learn tolerance of all paths, and just generally be "good people" is something they will carry with them all their lives, no matter their religious choice. This is the gift of a loving Wiccan home, and one which you began with a creative magickal spark that will never cease to burn in their hearts.

Gods and Goddesses for Pregnancy and Protection of Children

Bright Mother—the ovulating goddess

Brighid—Celtic goddess of childbirth and healing

Aphrodite—the embodiment of love and sex in Greek culture

Earth Mother—always depicted as pregnant

Althaea—Greek goddess of birth

Ama no Uzume—the Japanese Goddess whose dance became a fertility rite and a gift of life

Anat—Canaanite fertility image

Balit-ili—Babylonian protector of newborn children

Carmenta—Roman Goddess of childbirth

Chauturopayini—Hindu Goddess of fertility

Erce—Mother Earth and Fruitful Womb in Old English

Hera—Greek Goddess of maternity

Ilamatecuhtli—Aztec Goddess of fertility

Ishtar—Babylonian Goddess of marriage, love, and fecundity

Kahmden—Hindu mother Goddess

Mahueret—Egyptian Goddess of beginnings

Meshkent—Egyptian Goddess of childbirth and destiny

Ninmah—Chaldean Goddess of childbirth and motherhood

Nukua—Chinese creator and childbirth Goddess

Pihsia yuan chein—Chinese protector of mothers and children

Salus—Roman Goddess of health and welfare

Shakti—Hindu Goddess of creative power

Tuaret—Egyptian protector of mothers and children

Eros—Greek God of love and sexual desire

Assur—Assyrian God of fertility

Bes—Egyptian protector of women in childbirth

Dionysus—Greek God of fertility and fruitfulness

Ea—Chaldean husband to the Earth Goddess, God of water

Freyer—Scandinavian God of productivity

Holei—Japanese God of laughter and joy

Jizo Bosatsu—Japanese protector of childbirth and young

Lono—Polynesian fertility God

Narayana—Hindu God born from the primordial egg and whose name is sometimes associated with the egg itself

Sahur—Phoenician. Morning star of beginnings and sustenance.

Shiva—God of energy and preparation

Syen—Slavonic guardian spirits of the home

Upulero—Indonesian God of fecundity

*Xochipill*i—the Aztec flower prince who appeared in their fertility festivals as a God of romance and lover to the Moon.

ADDITIONAL RESOURCES

CASCADE BIRTHING, (800) 443-9942. Distributors of various books on birthing and alternative birth procedures.

BIOBOTTOMS, (800) 766-1254. Distributors of clothes, cloth diapers, and other earth-aware products for children.

NATURAL ELEMENTS, (408) 425-5448. Herbs, homeopathic remedies, natural vitamins, books.

MOONFLOWER BIRTHING SUPPLY, 2810 Wilderness Place #D, Boulder Colorado 80301. Everything!

EARTHTOOLS, (800) 825-6460. Environmentally aware home products company with catalogue.

HEARTHSONG, P.O. Box B, Sebastopol, California 95473. Books for Pagan parents, toys, craft supplies and kits, instruments.

MUSIC FOR LITTLE PEOPLE, P.O. Box 1460, Redway, California 95560. Musical instruments, tapes, language tapes and books.

SUGGESTED READING

Baldwin, Rahima. *Special Delivery.* Berkeley: Celestial Arts, 1986.

Budapest, Z. *Grandmother of Time.* San Francisco: HarperSan Francisco, 1989.

Colman, Arthur and Libby. *Earth Father/Sky Father.* New York: Prentice Hall, 1981.

Ehrenbach, Barbara, and Deirdre English. *Witches, Midwives, and Nurses: A History of Women Healers.* Old Westbury, New York: The Feminist Press, 1973.

Gaskin, Ina May. *Spiritual Midwifery.* Summertown, Tennessee: Book Publishing Co., 1989.

Jones, Carl. *Mind Over Labor.* New York: Viking Penguin, 1987

———. *Visualizations for Easier Childbirth.* Deephaven, Minnesota: Meadowbrook, 1988.

Jones, Carl and Jan. *The Birth Partner's Handbook.* New York: Simon and Schuster, 1989.

Kitzinger, Sheila. *The Complete Book of Pregnancy and Childbirth.* New York: Knopf, 1989.

———. *Homebirth.* New York: Dorling Kindersly, 1991.

Metzer, David, ed. *Birth: An Anthology of Ancient Texts, Songs, Prayers and Stories.* San Francisco: North Point Press, 1981.

Nobel, Elizabeth. *Essential Exercises for the Childbearing Year.* Boston: Houghton Mifflin, 1976.

Odent, Michel. *Birth Reborn.* New York: Pantheon, 1986.

————. *Entering the World: The De-Medicalization of Childbirth*. New York: Marion Boyers, 1989.

Willliams, Phyllis S., *Nourishing Your Unborn Child*. Los Angeles: Nash Publishing, 1974.

NOTES

[1]Having no visual beginning or ending, necklaces commonly symbolize the cycles of seasons, and more importantly the soul from birth, life, and death to rebirth.

[2]God/dess, spelled in this manner, is meant to represent both the male and female aspects of the divine image.

[3]The only time I do not recommend this approach is when you have had a history of difficult pregnancies or miscarriages. In this case it is emotionally safer to begin such practices after the first trimester, when chances of miscarriage have decreased.

[4]The Witches' Goddess is always depicted as having three aspects, the first of which is young and energetic and a maiden. The next aspect is the mother, who is older, ripe with fertility and full of loving care. Finally, the crone is the image of aged wisdom and eternal secrets. The God aspect of the Divine likewise is often shown with three images of boy, father, and grandfather.

[5]Smudging incense mixtures include sage and cedar to eliminate any negative energies and cleanse both individuals and the space.

ABOUT THE AUTHOR

Trish Telesco was born and raised in Buffalo, New York, where she was exposed to a variety of arts and chose poetry and theater as her early favorites. During high school and college she worked with the Pentacostal Assemblies of Canada as a missionary on various gospel-singing tours. After leaving the church, she lived in Boston, then returned to Buffalo where she began to study sacred geometry, dowsing, and leys. Later she founded a small magickal journal, *The Magi*, which she published until February 1992.

Trish is the author of two books, both available from Llewellyn Publications: *A Victorian Grimoire* and *The Urban Pagan*. She writes for a variety of Pagan publications. She considers herself a down-to-earth "kitchen Witch" who prefers spontaneous magicks to more formal approaches.

Now in her 30s, Trish has a 6-year-old son, five cats, and "a big dopey dog" named Ripley. Her hobbies include Celtic illumination, Sufi dancing, historical costume design, herbalism, wood and soapstone carving, singing, and brewing. She also operates a mail-order business dedicated to Earth-aware products. She and her husband are members of the Society for Creative Anachronism in which she has been honored for her work in herbalism, costuming, and music.

Thea Artemis Kinyon
Photo © 1993 Malcolm Brenner / Eyes Open

Raising a Pagan Child

by Karen Charboneau-Harrison

Bringing a new life onto this planet is a long-term commitment, and the challenges inherent in that commitment are multiplied a thousandfold when the child is raised a Pagan. Most of us live in the so-called Judeo-Christian culture: its values and judgments are present in everything we experience, sometimes openly and sometimes covertly.

This larger community assumes that everyone sees the world in a black-and-white, either/or way while ignoring diversity and options that can be explored and employed in living a fuller life. It assumes, too, that we have only one life to live, not many lives within which to learn our lessons, and that the rules promoted by dominant religions are "natural laws" rather than man-made ones. It assumes that all our information comes through the five physical senses and that "magic" is only Hollywood's special effects. It assumes we are all victims of "original sin" and without personal responsibility in the direction of our lives. It assumes children have no power in their own right, and, ultimately, that anything different from all these assumptions is suspect, threatening, frightening, or merely foolish.

The larger community celebrates and reinforces its world view in many ways. Holidays like Christmas and Easter, originally religious, are upheld by secular governments, for example. In the American Pledge of Allegiance, we pledge loyalty to a nation under one God: that God is not specifically designated as the Judeo-Christian Yahweh, but we all know who is being invoked.

While we Pagans abide by and support society's rules and regulations that make it possible for groups of people to live together, our world view is different from the dominant culture's because we differentiate between the laws of human society and the laws of the universe. The first set deal with questions and problems of community living, but universal laws explain the underpinnings of life experience and spiritual advancement. We view magick as a natural way to influence our environment, and we use it within a strong ethical framework. We regard our children as persons in their own right who strive just as adults do to understand their power and responsibility and to grow mentally, physically, emotionally, and spiritually. We see ourselves as part of the whole world, affecting the planet and each other but with no inherent right to rule Mother Earth or to determine the quality of life for her inhabitants.

Such basic differences in world view make Pagan parenting challenging and difficult. How do we guide our children wisely and nourish them spiritually in a culture that at best tolerates us and at its worst vilifies us? Harsh though it may sound, first we must accept that we are raising our children in an alien culture, one whose basic values conflict with ours. However, we are not the only ones in this predicament: there are Buddhist parents, traditional Native American parents, Hindu parents, and Muslim parents, all feeling their own degrees of alienation. And although the dominant culture claims to be based on "Judeo-Christian" concepts, Christian values predominate; therefore, Jewish parents face many of the same problems we do. Yet one difference is that parents of other religious traditions live within subcultures that are often more cohesive than their Pagan counterpart. The Jewish, Muslim, or Buddhist subcultures contain many friends and relatives following the same beliefs and customs. They recognize the need for cohesion and actively work to nurture and maintain it. They may not be totally understood by society at large, but they are usually not feared. Pagans, on the other hand, have centuries of "bad press" to combat, and we do not want our children on that battlefield. Depending on our circumstances, we may be the only Pagans in the area or the only Pagans with children in our community. This presents additional obstacles because we may feel we have no support. We have to work within our families to teach, celebrate, and reinforce our beliefs. Although the prospect may be daunting at times, we can create special learning experiences with our children and share with them their Pagan heritage without making them feel alien or strange.

Pagan parents must take this responsibility. Ours is a religion of this world, not one focused on an abstract afterlife. Utilizing everyday happenings to teach our ways can be one of our simplest, most effective tools. A Pagan parent must stay focused in the here-and-now in order to observe and teach her or his children about the inner and outer worlds they inhabit. One family can do this in its own home, but sometimes it is more fun and easier to organize a group of like-minded parents to develop a teaching plan. One group in Denver is attempting to do just that in an ambitious and organized fashion: Fortress Temple sponsors a Pagan "Sunday School" for children ranging from age five to teen-agers.

"With the influx of new adult students, we've found a need present for their children to be educated as well," said Judith Brownlee, high priestess of Fortress. "Initially, we wanted to present different Pagan paths as well as Wicca, but the people who came forward to help with the project were all Wiccan. We'll go with that for a while and see what happens."

Fortress Temple has developed a 13-week curriculum for each season. While the children are meeting in groups according to age (5–8, 9–12, and 13–18), interested parents meet in another room to compare notes, discuss problems, or just socialize.

Christmas and Easter can be confusing times for the Pagan family. Many Pagan parents came from Christian households, and they may fondly remember their earlier seasonal holiday rituals. Most of our Pagan children's friends will be celebrating these holidays, and our children can feel left out if we do not acknowledge these times too. By remembering that both Christmas and Easter are Pagan in origin and by celebrating the things they have in common in both traditions, we can have the best of both worlds and teach our children about the universality of religious expression.

Celebrate Yule with your children by telling the stories of the birth of the Sun child, why we have Yule trees, and the story of the Yule log. Sing the more Pagan-oriented carols ("Deck the Halls," for example) or change the words from the "traditional" ones. But start your celebration on the Winter Solstice. If you have relatives with whom you traditionally spend Christmas Eve or Christmas Day feasting and opening presents, start the season in your Pagan household by opening a gift each day beginning with the Solstice and culminating with Christmas.

Easter can be dealt with the same way. Talk about the beginnings of spring and how the traditions of Easter eggs, bunnies, and chicks originated. Plant some easy-sprouting seeds which can represent a child's wish. But do it on the Spring Equinox and follow up by giving your child a basket of goodies on Easter morning.

Halloween presents a different kind of problem. For us, it is one of our most sacred and important holidays, yet we are surrounded by green-faced, cardboard "witches" hanging over candy displays, plus offensive greeting cards. Story hour at school often involves a scary tale with a "witch" as the villain, and our children receive coloring handouts at school that depict at least one flying, warty "witch."

It is inappropriate to expect your child to challenge these misrepresentations or for you to arrive fuming at the school to confront the teacher or principal. Frustrating though it is to forego public confrontations, the proper response is to deal with these inconsistencies. Tell your children that these images are produced by people who do not really know anything about real Witches and that no hurt is intended. You can also explain how current North American Halloween customs began in order to show them how other people do celebrate an important holiday with us.

The need for discretion or secrecy can be a very confusing issue for the Pagan family. On one hand, much unnecessary difficulty can be avoided with a little discretion. On the other, explaining what is secret, what is not, and why it is so can make a parent feel like he or she has opened a can of very lively worms! Just as the family finances and Uncle Joe's belief that he is a being from Venus are family business not to be discussed with outsiders, our religious beliefs are "family business." Admittedly, this does get a bit sticky when we also advise the child not to talk to Grandma about it.

"Don't use the word 'secret,'" cautions Judith Brownlee of Fortress Temple. "It makes children want to talk about it for some reason. Use the word 'private.' Children understand about privacy, and you'll get better results."

Other parents handle this sensitive issue by not involving their children in Pagan religion at all. Melissa and John have two children, ages 10 and 13: "We feel that their late teens is early enough to explore any kind of religion. If they want to begin training for Wicca, we wouldn't start with our children any earlier than that anyway. They sometimes wonder what we're up to, but they just figure that it's their weird parents. We don't hide the fact that we are Witches from them. In this world, it's just easier for the kids not to have something that difficult to deal with until they are old enough."

Be aware that the younger the child, the more difficult it is to maintain secrecy, particularly with relatives. Right after my Wiccan friend Pauline had been handfasted, her three-year-old child was heard telling her new grandmother about her own Wiccaning rite:

"Morgan took off all my clothes, and they put me in the smoke. Then I saw the Goddess." Fortunately, Pauline had already talked with her new mother-in-law about her religious beliefs, so there were no repercussions, but the potential was there. Let Grandma take your child to her church: it will be a positive experience for both of them and give your child a firsthand experience of how other people worship. You can then show your child the common elements of Grandma's beliefs and your own while pointing out the aspects of your family's worship that Grandma may not be happy to hear about.

Just as you may need to be discreet about your religious affiliation at work, your child needs to be discreet at school. You can bet there will be playground discussions of religion and religious holiday observances that may leave your child feeling strange and excluded. Children are often cruel to people they perceive to be different from themselves. Your child may be subjected not only to the gibes of classmates but also have difficulty with teachers or administrators. You might even find yourself summoned to meet with the school social worker or psychologist. Lately there has been an upsurge in sensationalized accounts of "Satan worship" and "ritual abuse." (See the bibliography at the end of this article for specific reputable works in these areas.) Because of these largely unfounded concerns, you and your child run a risk of being investigated if you are public about your affiliation. For the sake of discretion, you may wish to use a fictitious name if, for example, you give television or newspaper interviews.

Your discussion of Paganism with your children can help them be able to discuss religion with others through the ways you explain Pagan concepts of spirituality and our holiday celebrations. Focusing on

Paganism's Earth-centered aspects will give children helpful information they can share with others. For instance, discussing our reverence for the Earth, our respect for animals and the environment, or how we worship by attuning our energies to the seasons can be helpful. While our Paganism is not identical to Native American ways, you may still point out parallels between Native respect for the Earth and our Pagan views so that your children can explain their beliefs using these examples. Caution your child to use words like "Earth religion" rather than "Paganism"; the word "Pagan" still has misleading or frightening connotations for unaware people. Discussing shared religious concepts such as the universal belief in an All-Creator and the need and desire to connect with and worship God/Goddess/Source on special religious occasions is also beneficial. If you understand other people's religious holidays, you will be able to explain their Pagan parallels. If your children are informed about other religions, they will be able to discuss religion with people of other persuasions by talking about how we do similar things. By focusing on parallels rather than the differences, you can impart to your children a respect for all forms of spiritual expression and defuse their feelings of being "different."

You can also make life easier for your children by teaching them about the general views of the prevailing culture rather than attempting to raise them in a vacuum. They will be exposed to it anyway in school, and some knowledge will prepare them. For example, during my childhood in Oklahoma I had one baby sitter who was a staunch Southern Baptist. My parents allowed her to take me to church with her on Sundays and to some other special events. I learned the basic beliefs of evangelical Christianity that way, and I have often been glad that I did. I now sometimes know what other people are thinking and how they arrived at their world view, and I can communicate with them more effectively. Since I already had a firm Pagan upbringing, my baby sitter's actions in no way infringed upon my beliefs but instead enlarged my understanding of the world around me.

One common Pagan belief is that all spiritual paths lead to the source and that individuals follow beliefs that allow them to communicate in their best way with Spirit. Therefore, it is in children's best interest to be introduced to different paths so that they may experience for themselves the vast diversity of spiritual expression. If you can, take them or see that they may visit a Sunday school, a synagogue, or a Buddhist temple, and then talk afterwards about the ways that all spiritual paths converge. Discuss in an open-minded way the differences between Paganism and the church or temple they just visited. You will learn a lot—and so will your child.

Beyond dealing successfully with the larger, alien culture in which we live, how can you teach your children about your religion?

Many covens with children feel that the Sabbats (in other words, the quarter and cross-quarter days) are the best time to introduce children to the ritual circle. Full and New Moons, on the other hand, are reserved for magickal workings by adults. In this view, since the Sabbats are more celebratory, children's participation in them is appropriate. Meanwhile, until the children are teen-agers, keep strictly magickal workings for adults only, so that you can concentrate on the ritual itself without having to worry about how your child is handling the energy. This is not to say that simple magickal technique and its foundations such as meditation should be off limits to children until their teen years. On the contrary, children should be encouraged to focus their energies and do simple rituals as long as they have been ethically prepared.

If your coven usually works skyclad (nude), it is a good idea to wear robes when doing ritual with children. Around age 7, children become very body-conscious. We live in a world where the nude body is regarded as unnatural, and this prevailing attitude could become just another battle to fight. Particularly as they begin puberty and their bodies begin to change, children are intimidated by the idea of other people seeing these changes. You can alleviate the tension by not making ritual nudity an issue. In addition, with all the problems of sexual abuse of children in the world, your child's mention of ritual nudity to outsiders could provoke an investigation. If parents are divorced and the custodial parent is Pagan, nudity could become a difficult issue should the non-custodial parent decide to question it in court.

In talking with young Pagans, I found that a chief idea they express is their desire for a structure within which to learn and experience the special qualities of Pagan religion.

"I sometimes would envy Christians for their big community-wide celebrations like Christmas. Everyone would be into the same thing together," said Morgan, 16. "I love it when our Pagan community comes together in a big circle and celebrates. It gives me a feeling of belonging."

Structure and community can be enhanced by incorporating young people's learning experiences into our Wheel of the Year. Several families with children can divide the teaching, which makes it less burdensome, but even within one family the cycles can be taught and enjoyed without too much trouble. Paganism, after all, is not just an intellectual discussion of abstract concepts but also includes experiential exploration no matter what the participants' ages. Take advantage of this in your teaching process. Include low-key ritual as part of the learning experience. Children enjoy chanting and dancing. I have never met a child who did not enjoy raising energy and sending it winging off into the universe. Plan rituals with children carefully. Keep the energy "soft" and leave lots of room within the framework for extemporaneous expression and experience. Talking about Wicca is fine, but the teaching becomes real within ritual.

Teaching Within the Wheel of the Year

The themes of the seasons can make planning easier. Spring brings new beginning and new growth. Summer is a time of work and of celebration to further the growth and accomplish our goals. Fall brings harvest of the growth and thanksgiving for the bounty. Winter is a time of slowing down and going within to discover our inner selves and to let go of the past. Utilize this framework to get ideas on what you want to present to your children and how to do it. Like most people, they will learn easiest and best by doing rather than by listening, so incorporating experiential lessons is important and makes learning more enjoyable. For example, to teach about opening up to one's psychic senses, you can play "Hide the Button" as part of the process. Hide a large button while the children close their eyes. Have them remain quiet inside and "feel" where it might be hidden.

Here are some suggestions for specific Pagan holidays. For additional material, see the chapter "Seasonal Rites/Magical Rites" in *Witchcraft Today, Book One: The Modern Craft Movement.*

SAMHAIN begins the Celtic New Year, the time when "the veil between the worlds is thin" and we are more sensitive to our inner selves and our psychic senses. The dead return to visit their old homes, and we can communicate with them to help them pass on and grow further. Seasonal rites celebrate the beginning of the rule of the God, Lord of the Underworld, and the Gate of Death. Our ancestors finished preserving their winter stores and began the slaughter of animals that would feed them throughout the winter. Magick is done at this time for the preservation through the winter months of the wild animals and winter food stores and to strengthen the Sun for his rebirth at Yule.

Some suggestions for Samhain celebrations including children might include the following:

- Perform divinations for the coming year.
- Make dream pillows (see below).
- Carve pumpkins.
- Make masks (see below).
- Talk about relatives or friends who have passed on and what we learned from them or enjoyed about them.
- Tell stories about ghosts, using the stories to illustrate how children might deal with fears.
- Talk about the origin of Halloween customs. Trick or treating goes back to the beginning of the Iron Age when farm dwellers left offerings of milk, cheese, or other treats to discourage the forest dwellers from pilfering. Costume parties

developed during the Middle Ages so that on Halloween ("hallow" or holy evening) the active ghosts and goblins could not recognize the people inside their homes celebrating the new year and therefore could not bother them. Jack-o'-lanterns developed from the custom of carving out turnips and placing candles in them to prevent the wind from blowing out the flame when people traveled at night.

YULE celebrates the rebirth of the Sun child and focuses on sending out energy to ensure that the rebirth occurs. Most modern Christmas customs are modified old Pagan customs. Decorating one's home with evergreen plants symbolizes undying life and the optimism that life will return after winter's harshness. Our ancestors believed that, by decorating with evergreen plants such as holly, ivy, and mistletoe, they were helping to bring the Sun through a dangerous time of diminished light.

Some suggestions for celebrating Yule:

- Decorate a tree after discussing with your children why we bring green things into our homes at this time.
- With agricultural chores at their minimum, our ancestors used winter for handicrafts. Likewise, you may make your own tree decorations of strung cranberries, popped corn (corn being a symbol of the God), and other homemade items.
- Make your own gifts for one another.
- Tell stories about the Sun child. The newborn baby Dionysus is one example: He is shown in Pompeian frescoes lying in a harvest basket on the threshing floor with a golden nimbus glowing from his head.

- Sing seasonal songs such as "Deck the Halls" and slightly modify Christian songs such as "Silent Night."
- Tell stories about the origins of Yule customs. For example, the Yule-log custom is widespread in Europe and was carried to some communities and homes in North America. A huge oak or pine log was brought into the house during the Yule season and kindled in the belief that the fire would protect the inhabitants from lightning, fires, and sickness. During the rest of the year a piece was kept under a bed to continue the protection; it was also dipped in water that was then sprinkled into the cattle's water to help them calve. The next year's Yule fire was lit from the old Yule log and the ashes kept to be mixed in with the spring seed to promote growth. Traditionally, writing one's wishes on a piece of paper and burning it with the Yule log on Solstice Eve makes them come true.

Holly represents death and rebirth and is sacred to Mother Holle, a Scandinavian goddess of death and regeneration. Its white flowers symbolize death and purification, the red berries rebirth and physical life, and the deep green leaves everlasting life.

Our ancestors venerated mistletoe because it grows upon the sacred oak and remains green in winter when the oak is bare of leaves. It was thought that the mistletoe guarded the oak's soul during winter's harshness. The custom of kissing beneath the mistletoe came from the idea that the mistletoe is the regenerative force of the God and, when one kisses another underneath it, one is wishing life and luck for one's partner.

Santa Claus or Kris Kringle comes from the Norse traditions. During the Yule season's stormy nights, Odin rides his eight-footed horse throughout the world bestowing gifts on worthy people and dispensing justice to transgressors. Kris Kringle ("Christ of the Wheel") is the title of the Norse god born at Winter Solstice.

OIMELC or **IMBOLG** is a time of purification and preparation for new life that will come in the spring. In the Catholic calendar it is known as St. Brigit's day or Candlemas. Oimelc marks the first stirrings of life in the earth. The custom of blessing and burning candles signifies the awakening life force and honors the goddess Brigit, for fire is sacred to her.

Consider these possibilities for celebrating Oimelc:

- Carry out rites of candle purification (and, symbolically, self-purification).
- Burn a figure of Winter to signify the end of harsh weather and old ways.
- Burn the mistletoe, holly, and ivy decoration from Yule to burn away the old and keep the goblins from the house.
- Wassail the trees and each other: prepare a spiced apple cider and drink to each other's health. At midnight go out among the trees and drink to their fruitfulness; then pour the cider on their roots and dance among the trees.
- Twelfth Night customs are appropriate here. Bake a cake and hide a bean in one portion. Whoever gets the bean becomes the king or queen of the feast, commanding each person to do something silly—and these commands must be obeyed.

- Appoint one person to "awaken the earth" during the ritual. He or she goes to the ritual circle's north quarter and beats upon the ground, calling out to Mother Earth to wake up.
- A party with masks and dancing is appropriate at this time (like Mardi Gras) to celebrate getting through the winter and to celebrate the new life on its way.

OSTARA or Spring Equinox sees light and darkness balanced but light gaining in power. It is the beginning of the agricultural year, and its rites ensure the revival of vegetation and the fertility of the flocks. The God and Goddess begin their courtship.

Some suggestions for celebrating Ostara:

- Spring cleaning is appropriate. Clear out old clothes, books, toys, and other items and give them away to make room for the new.
- Dye eggs as symbols of new beginnings and new life.
- Explain the Easter bunny's origins to your children. The hare or rabbit is sacred to Diana/Artemis. We all know how fertile rabbits are: they represent the fertility that is beginning. When the bunny brings gifts of eggs, it is bringing the gift of renewal.
- Have a sunrise observance.
- Bless some seeds with a wish. Plant them, and as they come up, the wish is fulfilled.
- Write and perform a mystery play about the God's resurrection. Write one about Ishtar and Tammuz or Isis and Osiris.
- If you bought a live Yule tree, now is the time to plant it.

BELTANE celebrates both the union of the God and Goddess and the beginning of the fertile Goddess's rule. Now we can see and experience the power of her abundance in the growing, flowering vegetation around us and the softly warm days.

Some celebrations for celebrating Beltane:

- Erect a Maypole (symbol of the God's fertile power) and decorate it with ribbons and flowers. Enjoy yourselves weaving a dance with the ribbons around the pole.
- Decorate May baskets with flowers and fruits to give to others.
- Go out at sunrise and wash your face in the morning dew.
- Build a small bonfire and jump over it to stimulate fertility of the body or the mind.
- Make flower wreaths from your garden to wear in your hair.
- Make May wine: buy a bottle of inexpensive chablis and decant it into a larger jar or bottle. Add a handful of woodruff and chamomile and let the herbs steep until Litha (see below), shaking the bottle each day. Strain and enjoy. You can do the same thing with apple juice, but you must keep it refrigerated during the steeping process.
- Have an outdoor party with a May King and Queen. Let them preside over the celebration of Maypole dancing, races, and games.

LITHA or Summer Solstice celebrates the Sun at the height of his power. It includes elements of fire and water for the marriage of the God and Goddess and to acknowledge the need at this time for the Sun and the rain to help the crops grow.

Celebrations may include such elements as these:

- Play under a lawn sprinkler.
- Paint each other with water-soluble paints.
- Decorate your front door with birch boughs, fennel, and roses.
- Have a picnic in a city park and bring boats to sail on the pond.
- Bless some water and then water the plants you planted at Ostara.
- Take an herb walk and identify growing herbs.

LUGHNASSADH or Lammas is a first-fruits celebration honoring the Sun god Lugh, ripener of grains. The rites at this time thank Him for His gifts and serve to avert storms that could destroy the crops. It is a time to bless the garden, the beehives, and the harvest tools.

A Lughnassadh celebration could include these elements:

- If you have a well or spring in your area, bless it and decorate it with flowers and ivy.
- Harvest the first crops from your garden and dedicate them to the Old Gods. If you don't have a garden, take a trip to a local farmer's market and purchase some vegetables and fruits to dedicate.
- Bake some bread.
- Make a corn dolly. Remove the husks from three ears of corn. Fashion them into the image of a woman with full skirts. Decorate your altar with it. Another type of corn dolly, based on the old meaning of "corn" as any small grain, can be woven from ears of wheat, etc. Handicraft books and magazines often carry instructions.

- Have a singing contest.
- Float some flowers at your local creek.

MABON or Autumn Equinox is the Harvest Home and is a time of thanksgiving for all that has been accomplished and learned throughout the year. It is a time of bidding farewell to summer and of honoring the family and friendship bonds.

Mabon celebrations for children may include the following:

- Let each member tell a story about a personal accomplishment during the year.
- Have a thanksgiving feast.
- Can and preserve produce.
- Bring in flowers and produce from the home garden to bless, being sure to leave some flowers and produce as a thanks to Mother Earth.
- In Roman and Celtic cultures the God either has been sacrificed at Lughnassadh or is at this time. For young children, a symbolic sacrifice enactment can be a bit much. To maintain the theme without upsetting the children, you can break bread in the form of the God, and as you break the bread and partake of it, talk about the idea of self-sacrifice for the good of all, or enact the myth of Dionysus wherein the young God is abducted as winter begins to return at the Winter Solstice.

We parents should not fall into the trap of insisting that our children follow in our spiritual footsteps. Our faith does not preach that it is the One, True, and Only Way. You may have a child who responds spiritually to another path. As long as she or he is following something that provides strength and guidance, it does not really matter what the name of it is. As your child explores other religions, he or she may adhere to one or another for a short time or a long time. So what? I am sure that you do not want your child feeling coerced into practicing any religion, including yours.

Sometimes when children are young, they are enthusiastic about family traditions but at puberty they become focused on music or friends. This too is natural. They may return to Paganism later after having satisfied the need to learn where they stand in the outside world. What is essential to impart to your children is a solid spiritual foundation; leave it up to them to decide the appropriate structure.

One of the gifts of parenting is that by teaching one's children and answering their questions, we learn more about ourselves and discover any hypocrisy or confusion within ourselves and our beliefs. In bringing up our children, we often rediscover how magickal the world really is and get the chance to relive childhood. As we teach our children about diversity and honoring spirituality, we can enjoy those aspects in the people around us. Raising a Pagan child is a challenge but is more than compensated for by the rapid growth the parent receives in his or her own development. In answering all of the "why" questions and gently unfolding the mysteries of life and death to a young person, one sees through a child's wondering eyes again, and this in itself is a passage to rebirth.

Suggestions for Activities According to Age Groups

Sabbat celebrations are appropriate for any age group if you keep in mind that small children have short legs, so fast circle dancing can be awkward. Telling stories about the legends surrounding each Sabbat prior to the ritual or as part of the ritual's beginning helps the children to focus and makes the event more meaningful and fun.

Doing activities together that teach a lesson about the stewardship of our Earth make our religion more meaningful also. Herb walks, park cleanup activities, and recycling can be productive and fun family activities.

Psychic-development activities can be fun for children. Cut colored construction paper into small pieces and hold a piece in your hand to hide the color. Have the children quiet themselves and concentrate on what color they "feel" is in your hand. When the telephone rings, ask who the caller is before answering it. Think of an animal, number, or color and have the children guess what it is. Let them in turn think of the animal, number, or color and learn to concentrate to project the information.

Make a habit of discussing dreams in the mornings. Talk about what the different symbols or events in the dreams might mean.

Use short guided meditations to introduce children to their personal inner voices or guides. Have them ask these inner voices for help with personal problems and discuss with them the answers they receive.

Teach them to "breathe" color or energy. For example, on a summer day, go outdoors and have them concentrate on and feel the touch of the Sun on their skin. Tell them to breathe slowly and rhythmically, 1–2–3–4, and begin to imagine that the Sun's warmth and energy is entering their lungs with each breath. Tell them to breathe out tension or worry with each exhalation. Indoors, you can put a colored light bulb in a socket and then have them sit near or under the light and do a similar exercise. Discuss how each part of the body feels when the particular color is "breathed" there. On days when a child is not feeling well, tell him or her to imagine breathing in the Sun's energy and putting it into that body area that does not feel well. Alternately, suggest breathing in the color blue to soothe the afflicted area.

When a pet dies, take the opportunity to discuss death and reincarnation with your child. Put together a simple passing ritual with them.

Create other simple rituals to commemorate different passages or important events in your child's life such as starting school, important decisions or lessons learned, puberty, or broken friendships.

Enroll your child in an open Sunday School! Many Unitarian churches have very open Sunday School curricula that explore different religious paths, including Pagan and Native American.

Activities Specific to Age Group

- 1–3 years: Storytelling, singing, reading stories, dancing to music or drumming.
- 4–7 years: Draw pictures of magickal animals, people, and places and color them while making a story about the picture. Read books such as the Serendipity series. Park cleanup (with supervision), creating songs or chants, dancing to music or drumming, dream-telling and analysis, beginning psychic exercises, color and energy breathing, passage rituals, baking (with supervision) cookies for the Sabbat.
- 8–11 years: All of the above, plus stargazing, meditation exercises, discussions of different aspects and cultural experiences of the God and Goddess.

- 12–15 years: All of the above, plus you may begin teaching a specific and simple divination tool such as pendulum or tea-leaf gazing; discussions regarding ethics and magick; creating ritual—have them put together a ritual which the family does together; basic astrology.
- 16–18 years: If you get this age group to slow down long enough, you will be lucky. Discussions of magick and ethics, sexuality and ethics, and the power of magick can sometimes engage their interest. Beginning a more advanced divination technique such as Tarot is appropriate if interest warrants. Many people in this age group are interested in various "rights" groups such as animal rights, Native American rights, or ecology, and these may be encouraged from a Pagan perspective.

Mask Making

Supplies:
Plaster of Paris strips (Buy these at an art or
    medical supply store.)
Vaseline or other petroleum jelly
Bowl of water
Plastic straws
Water-based paints
Decorations such as feathers and beads
Glue

Cut the plaster strips into three-inch lengths. Lay approximately ten strips in the water bowl. Cover the subject's face with a thin layer of Vaseline so that the plaster of Paris won't adhere to the skin. Place protection over the eyes (eye makeup removal pads work well), and put a short straw in each nostril so the subject can breathe.

Beginning with the forehead, place the strips on the face, contouring them to the face's shape. Go on to the sides of the face and chin, building inwards over the nose. Add more strips to the water bowl as needed. Do the eye area last, since it is the trickiest. You may also chose to make a half-mask, forming the strips over the cheeks and nose but leaving the mouth and chin free. A half-mask allows for eating, drinking, and speaking clearly. If your child wears glasses, you can shape the mask over the glasses while the child is wearing them so that they are incorporated into the mask but underneath it.

When you are satisfied with the shape of the mask, remove it carefully from the face and set it somewhere safe to dry for 24 hours. When the mask is thoroughly dry, you can paint it with acrylic or other water-based paint, glue beads and feathers onto it, or hang lightweight objects like ribbons from it.

True Dream Pillow

Supplies:
Cotton or silk material
Any or all of these herbs: Lavender flowers, anise pieces, mugwort, jasmine flowers, white sandalwood, lily of the valley, lilac flowers, chamomile, hops, skullcap, poppy seeds
Essential oils of any of the above herbs
Needle and thread to sew the edges or ribbon to tie material

Cut a piece of material to the size you desire the pillow to be. You will want your pillow to be no smaller than four inches square. In the center of the piece of cloth, place your herb and oil mixtures: for the four-inch-square piece, use about one-fourth cup. For larger pillows, place enough herb mixture to fill but not overflow your material.

To prepare the herb-oil mixture, mix equal parts of each of the herbs desired, beginning with one tablespoon of each, to get an idea of the volume of the final mixture. When you have reached the volume you need, begin adding oils to the center of the dry herbs a few drops at a time. Knead the oils in gently with a spoon until the scent is as strong as you like.

If you are sewing the pillow, fold it in half and sew the cut sides together with a slip stitch. You may want to sew some ribbon or cord to one corner if you wish to hang it rather than keeping it on the bed.

For those who would rather not sew, lay the material flat with the herb mixture in the center. Take two opposing corners and bring them together. Do the same with the remaining two corners. Packing the herb mixture tightly in the middle, twist the corners up together and bind them with a ribbon.

Dream pillows can be used to help remember dreams or to ease dreams in the case of children with nightmares.

Additional Resources

THE EDUCATION FOR PAGAN YOUTH COM-
MITTEE (EPYC), headed by Judith Brownlee, is a Pagan
"Sunday school" in Denver, Colorado, for children ages
4 to 18. It provides a broad Pagan religious education,
allows Pagan children to meet each other, and allows
Pagan parents to learn that they are not alone and to
support one another.

The curriculum is divided quarterly and is based
on the Wheel of the Year.

Suggested Movies for Pagan Children

Emerald Forest, 1985
Fern Gully, 1992
Labyrinth, 1986
Legend, 1986
Legend of Ra, 1990*
Neverending Story, 1984
Sorceress, 1983*
Star Wars trilogy, 1977, 1980, 1983

---

*Available from Mystic Fire Videos, P.O. Box 9323, Dept. C5,
South Burlington, Vermont 05407.

SUGGESTED READING

BELLEROPHON COLORING BOOKS, 36 Anacape St., Santa Barbara, California 93101. A series of wonderful coloring books whose subjects range from American Indians to King Tut.

DOVER BOOKS, publisher of inexpensive and extensive titles. For catalog write to Dover Books, 31 E. 2nd St., New York, New York 11501, specifying children's books.

THE WORLD MYTHOLOGICAL SERIES. New York: Schocken Books. This series combines a good text and wonderful illustrations to cover Greek, Norse, Chinese, American Indian, South American, Roman, Arab, Russian, Celtic, and other mythologies.

Other Books

Edwards, Carolyn M. *Story Teller's Goddess.* San Francisco: HarperSan Francisco, 1991

Phelps, E. *Maid of the North.* New York: Holt, Rinehart & Winston, 1981

Slade, Paddy. *Encyclopedia of White Magic.* New York: Mallard Press/Bantam, 1990.

Strichartz, Naomi. *The Wise Woman.* New York: Cranehill Press, 1986

———— *The Wise Woman's Sacred Wheel of the Year.* New York: Cranehill Press, 1986

Periodicals

H.A.M. (How About Magic?) is a magazine written for and by magickal children. Published by Green Egg,

P.O. Box 1542, Ukiah, California 95483. Subscriptions: United States via first-class mail, $7. Canada and Latin America via first class mail, in envelope, $9. Europe via air mail, in envelope, $9. Japan and Australia via air mail, in envelope, $10.

Additional Bibliography

Graves, Robert. *The White Goddess*. New York: Farrar, Strauss and Giroux, 1948

Hicks, Robert. *In Pursuit of Satan: The Police and the Occult*. Buffalo: Prometheus Books, 1991

LaChapelle, Dolores, and Janet Bourque. *Earth Festivals*. Silverton, Colorado: Finn Hill Arts, 1973.

Mercer, Joyce. *Behind the Mask of Adolescent Satanism*. Minneapolis: Deaconness Press, 1991. (Written from a Christian perspective, but still a level-headed look at why some teens are attracted to what they perceive as Satanism and "black magic.")

ABOUT THE AUTHOR

Born 31 October 1954, Karen Charboneau-Harrison is an author, priestess, lecturer, and owner of Moon Magick, a small company making ritual herbal products. She has been involved in fields of metaphysics and Pagan spirituality since her childhood, having been fortunate to grow up in a like-minded family.

She is the mother of a 17-year-old, independent-thinking daughter who intensively trained her in the needs and challenges of growing up Pagan. She and her husband, Jeff, have enjoyed the opportunity to experience creative parenting firsthand.

Karen has been a member of MoonFire Coven since 1979 and has also been active since 1969 in dispelling negative images of Witches, speaking at high schools, colleges and universities, in the news media, and wherever else she can. She serves as a liaison between Denver-area Pagans and law enforcement agencies, holds in-service programs for mental healthcare practitioners, law enforcement, and school administrators. She helped found Women's Spiritual Leadership Alliance, a group of women leaders and teachers who meet regularly to share their expertise with one another for the purposes of networking, mutual empowerment, and community work.

Zack Darling

Between the Worlds

Late Adolescence and Early Adulthood in Modern Paganism

by Anodea Judith

Adolescence is a challenging time in the best of worlds. Neither adult nor child, the adolescent is caught betwixt and between the worlds of autonomy and dependence, freedom and constriction, power and powerlessness. Not only is this stage confusing and difficult for all concerned, but cultural demands extend its duration. With the lengthy time required for higher schooling and the difficulty of finding one's way in a complex world, adolescence can now last 10 to 15 years.

Adolescent rebellion may be a stereotype, but is it a natural, healthy stage of breaking away from parental dependency or is it a reaction to outdated and repressive values? How much of adolescent rebellion is developmental and how much is culturally determined? How much do rites of passage practiced in other societies have an effect on their adolescents' adjustment to adulthood? How does one's religious upbringing affect the young adult entering the world at this tumultuous and confusing time?

To explore some of these questions from a Pagan perspective, I interviewed three young adults, aged 16–22, who were raised by Pagan parents in and around a Pagan and Nature-oriented community. I wanted to know how they defined themselves spiritually, how they felt about their Pagan upbringing, and whether they saw a Pagan spiritual perspective as continuing to play a role in their future, as well as exploring some of the questions raised above.

Aside from the interviews, the profiles of their lives speak strongly about their Pagan heritage:

Lasara Firefox, age 20, was raised in a rural community in Northern California. Her experience is unique, and to many may seem extreme. Third child of six, Lasara was raised on 80 acres of near wilderness, living in hand-built houses with no electricity or telephones and dirt roads of questionable quality. The land is part of a larger community of parcels owned by people with countercultural values who left the city during the 1970s "back to the land movement" to find a better way of life. Many of these parcels of land are Pagan-owned and there is a strong Pagan community with which her parents (especially her mother) were associated. I myself have known Lasara since she was four and often visited her family's home in the hot summer to see her red hair flying over her partially clothed body as she ran through the fields with her siblings.

Lasara was also home-schooled, both for practical and philosophical reasons, as her mother disagreed with the public school system's "indoctrination," and getting through the miles of muddy roads in the winter was often impossible. At the time of the interview,

Lasara was 20 years old and six months into her year's reign as May Queen, an office of high magical honor, bestowed on her by the local community's Beltane rites.

Lasara feels that growing up on the land gave her a basic Pagan world view—an understanding of being in Nature that was fundamental to her existence. I asked her how she might state her beliefs at this time.

"I believe in the Earth as a nurturing force. Magic is metaphor—directing energy in the form of an image and changing the existing structure of things. A lot of Paganism is imagery. It's beautiful images for a plain truth. It's real; it's something I can touch and smell and feel."

At 12, she started her own research into magical customs, trying to find information on the things that surrounded her such as the magical use of local plants or the the symbolic nature of certain trees. Each summer her family held a ten-day "drama camp" for children, giving her a wonderful background for participation in dramatic ritual. In 1986, at age 14, she and her younger siblings went with their mother on the Peace March, walking across the entire United States. On the march she was exposed to many rituals and many different faiths, yet still chooses to call herself Pagan when asked by someone who understands the true meaning of the word—one who worships and honors Nature, the seasonal cycles, and the dance of the God and Goddess.

Zack Darling, 16, son of an editor of the well-known Pagan publication *Green Egg*, has been raised in and around Paganism as well as Buddhism in his early life. Feeling "Proud to be Pagan" (his final statement to me in our interview), he is thankful for the unique philosophical understanding he has. Most valuable to him has been his exposure to the animal world. Having been raised around animals all his life—raising snakes, rats, ferrets, goats, unicorns, owls, pheasants, cats, rabbits, tarantulas, and iguanas—he has chosen to become a zookeeper and work with endangered species, for he feels a deeply spiritual value in the animal realm.

Zack believes the Pagan world view is important for children but hard for a child to understand, due to the esoteric language of adults spiritually pontificating during their social gatherings. So he started the publication *HAM (How About Magic),* as a youth-oriented adjunct to *Green Egg. HAM* publishes articles by and for Pagan youth about ritual, mythology, politics, and sexuality. After nine quarterly issues (at the time of the interview), Zack is emerging as a young Pagan leader of considerable merit.[1]

Rainbow (her given though not current name) is 22, daughter of an prominent Pagan priestess and a Buddhist father. At 22, Rainbow defines herself as a Pagan, although her personal style is quieter than her mother's more dramatic public persona. Rainbow feels most thankful for her Pagan upbringing as she witnesses the spiritual and moral crises of her friends.

"I feel like they are just beginning to grasp truths about life, God, and sexuality that were basic to me as far back as I can remember. While they are confused and trying to sort it all out, I feel I have a religion that makes sense. So my friends come to me for an alternate opinion."

Rainbow differs from Zack and Lasara in that she left Paganism for awhile, returning to it on her own a few years later. I asked her about the influences behind these changes:

"I think a lot of it was because I wanted to deny my whole hippie upbringing. I just didn't want to think about it. It was hard for me because my Mom was always so intense about bombarding me, trying to prepare me through my youth and not letting me do it on my own. So I pushed it away because she had it in my face all the time."

I asked how long she pushed it away and about the influences that made her come back:

"I don't know exactly—maybe seven years or so. What made me come back was looking at environmental issues and that really sums it up. It's more immediate. You see this pain in front of you daily. I think a lot of that brought me around—looking at the planet Gaia and realizing that we really need to wake up! It made me want to connect on a deeper basis and contribute to the healing instead of being part of the problem."

The Pagan world view of worshiping the Earth Mother as a living entity, of respecting the biosphere and its diversity of plants, animals, and varied human culture, speaks to the dilemmas our children will be facing as they inherit a world already ravaged and plundered. They need a philosophy that addresses these issues rather than ignoring them.

In her recent book *Behind the Mask of Adolescent Satanism,* Joyce Mercer describes the reasons some adolescents turn to that dangerous path.

Teen Satanism arises to fill a void, to meet unfulfilled needs of young people ...who seek ways to express the great, intangible aspects of life with which they come into contact—forces of love and hatred, a greater sense of purpose or meaning, devotion to a cause or ideal, questions of ethics and values, the ability to identify with other people and feel compassion, and a sense of connection or community. These are the spiritual concerns of young people. When healthy, positive spirituality is absent, young people will seek other ways to address their spiritual needs.[2]

Without a sense of personal power, without connection to meaningful symbols, without a world view that addresses the realities a young teen faces, whether they be sexuality or environmental disaster, teens can act out their frustration in crime or Satanic activities. Paganism offers a healthy alternative—one that gives teens a sense of their own power, gives them a world rich with symbols, and addresses the issues that they must face in their future.

However, revived Paganism is still in its youthful stage, and I knew there would also be many pitfalls. With the exception of the rare hereditary witch in the parent's age group, our current youth is the first modern generation to grow up under Pagan values. This puts Pagan children in a religious minority among their peers, and I wondered if they were ostracized or ridiculed as they were growing up.

Zack replied, "Just about always, but not for being Pagan, because I never really advertised my beliefs. I only told my friends whom I trusted. Now that I'm in high school I have more friends that wear crystals and all and no longer write this kind of stuff off as Satanism. I even have friends from other religions who are really interested."

Lasara had a similar experience: "I was considered weird as a child, but it wasn't because I was Pagan. It was just me. I was raised on the ranch, I was home-schooled. I was a poor child, and that always makes a child weird. The Paganism wasn't visible. The poverty was."

Rainbow, aside from having a certain stigma attached to her name, was also quiet about her beliefs. She now feels her difference most strongly in the form of being hypersensitive to the prejudice and oppression of Pagan belief systems. "When Christians get up in my face, telling people what to believe, I get really upset. Even in my college philosophy of religion course, it was almost entirely about Christian philosophers—when there are so many other opinions. Or the way Pagans are sometimes portrayed in movies. I really get angry about that, but people don't always understand why it bothers me so much."

Rainbow has spent time on her own studying the Huna tradition of spirituality, but felt that the people she studied with were caught up in "New Age" ideology which lacked the down-to-earth quality so important to her.

One noticeable difference between Pagan attitudes and those from other religions is around sexuality. Pagans revere sexuality as a sacred act of God and Goddess and as a celebration of our bodies and our life force. How does growing up in an environment with nudity, permissive sexuality, and deities of both genders affect the budding sexuality of the young Pagan?

As one might expect, the answer was different from female to male. Rainbow feels that she currently has very healthy attitudes about sex, without the guilt and fear that she sees in some of her peers. She resented however, what felt to her like pressure as she was growing up to become "liberated," and her current sexuality is basically monogamous. She believes in one's right to make their own choice, but sees the sexual freedom revolution as imposing expectations upon people to be more active than they might want. "I just don't think people at my age are mature enough to handle that."

Lasara also commented on the change in her relation to the community after her "coming of age" ritual at 18. "Suddenly, there they were, waiting in line, now that I was officially no longer a child. That amount of attention that passes as worship of the Goddess has given me a reverse reaction: that it's never okay to say yes. If I said yes to one, I feel there would be an expectation to sleep with the others."

Lasara is currently in a monogamous relationship, living with a man for the first time in her life (who reigns with her this year as May King). And despite her resentment of the sexual pressure, she feels children should be exposed to sexuality. She did not agree with the community's decision to have a separate ritual for the younger children while the sexually playful "May games" were being held.

"My views on sex are different than most people. I grew up naked, around nudity and sexuality. I want to make children unafraid of sex, to help them think of it as what it is—a creation, a fire, a beautiful flower blossoming, a union of male and female, God and Goddess. That's what lovemaking is. The May games were healthy, playful. Children should see that."

As a male, Zack had very little to say against the open sexuality. "I think it helped me gain a lot more respect towards women. It made me have an attitude that was so much more positive about sex than the kids I would go to school with and grow up with who weren't Pagan. Instead of sex being a bad thing, which is the attitude Christian kids get, it gave me a lot more respect and honor for someone's needs, and what would be honest and caring. A lot of what I feel is in the article I wrote for *HAM* about youth and maiden lovemaking."[3]

In the article Zack addresses issues of sexuality and responsibility for young teens. He covers the obvious things, such as sexually transmitted diseases, condoms, and pregnancy, but also writes about equally important points, such as respecting someone's right to say no, without arguing or pushing for more, respecting your partner's privacy ("Don't go brag to all your friends about it. Keep it between you."). He writes of "outercourse," or non-penetrative lovemaking, as a way to enjoy contact without risk. Some adults reacted critically to Zack's article, feeling that talking about sex to teens gives the impression that minors are encouraged to have sex. The article, however, clearly addressed the issues of age, and the need to consider the ethical and legal responsibility of avoiding sexual play with younger partners. Zack's intention was for the article to promote positive attitudes towards sex and encourage responsibility and consideration on the part of young people who are going to experiment anyway. I know that in reading it I certainly wished the boys in my high school 20 years ago had had a few of those concepts under their belts!

In these instances, Pagan sexual attitudes have successfully promoted healthy and responsible sexual behavior while preserving an understanding of its sacred nature. There is a warning here, however, to avoid going too far in the direction of countercultural permissiveness, always remembering to let the delicate nature of one's sexuality unfold at its own pace and style. True sexual freedom means allowing each person to define themselves, according to their own inner being. Pressure to perform can be as unpleasant as the inhibition of one's enjoyment.

In many non-Christian cultures, adolescence is marked by a ritual of passage. I asked my young friends if anything like that had been done for them and how they felt about it.

Rainbow replied that her mother had wanted to do that for her at the time of her first blood, but that she adamantly declined. "I'd rather have a root canal! I didn't want to be the focal point. I feel I'm more of a spectator. I know the concept 'Thou Art Goddess' implies a certain worshiping of yourself, but it's a hard step for me. I don't necessarily like the whole ego aspect. It gives us humans too much importance." She feels the egotism of humans is at least part of the reason why we have polluted the world so mercilessly.

Instead Rainbow's most powerful spiritual experiences occurred through the continuing tree plantings and participation in "Redwood Summer," a recent attempt on the part of environmentalists to alter the logging practices used against the ancient old-growth redwood forests. Throughout the summer, community camps were held in the spirit of nonviolence, using political tactics of demonstration, ritual, negotiation, and peer support. "That's been something that brought it home to me—that this is serious. Also, going out and spending time by myself in the woods, I have a kind of spiritual 'at peace' feeling."

Zack's most powerful spiritual experience occurred quite by accident. At 15, Zack was working under a truck, and it slipped off the jacks, violently slamming his head and pinning him under the car. It pushed the breath out of his chest and the weight kept him from taking another. His stepfather, by an heroic miracle of strength, was able to lift the car in the nick of time. "During those moments, I saw my life pass before me. I really thought I was done for. I thought of the people I loved and cared for. I wanted to be able to tell my mother that I loved her. I wanted so much to live. Everything since then has had a different flavor. I am so grateful for the colors and sounds, the life I have been given. It changed me profoundly, and was my most powerful spiritual experience."

Zack did have a planned coming-of-age ritual at 13. "I felt that the rite of passage let me into the men's circle and the whole male aspect of magic. But I never really felt I was a man until the truck fell on me. My rite of passage didn't do that, even though it was supposed to. I just knew I wouldn't really be risking death during the rite because it was people I trusted."

Lasara's rite of passage occurred at 18, and I was fortunate enough to be present. The ritual occurred as part of a larger seasonal celebration and was attended by the whole community. She was birthed naked through a large "yoni gate" made of twisting oak branches laced with flowers, presented to her community with her new name, and given gifts and robes while being honored with songs and poetry. Her brother, Emrys, was also honored two years later, at 13, with a similar ritual, after passing his ordeal the night before of drumming a constant heartbeat rhythm for the dusk to dawn Walpurgisnacht ritual. At his celebratory rites the next day, he appeared in a robe he had made himself, with a cloak of leather that he had tanned himself. He was presented to the community as having passed his test, and was given gifts and honored with words of wisdom from his elders.

These adolescents did not appear to have gone through the usual rebellion stage. Their relationship to their parents was good. There was friendship, support, and trust. None felt a need to avoid his or her parents, but instead enjoyed their company as well as the company of other adults, and of course, friendship with their peers. Is this something different for Pagan youth that says more about our culture than it does about adolescence?

Rainbow says she still rebelled. "I went for a different scene. I just found something that I knew (my Dad) would dislike—heavy metal, head-banger scenes. My Mom was cool about it though, and she used to go to concerts with me. That was the good thing about her being so open-minded. She's always been like my best friend, but not like my Mom. It's hard when I want a Mom instead, though it's less of an issue now. But when I was growing up it was really painful. I wanted her to be there, to call, to check up on me more."

Zack, who also likes heavy metal, radical hair styles, and other emblems of today's youth, finds it hard to rebel against something so good. "If you rebel, what are you going to do? Go to church? Why do that when you can meet Gods and Goddesses and skinny-dip in the pond? I think the main thing Pagan kids can find to rebel against is the health food!"

His mother, a single mother most of his life, was strict with him at times. "My Mom's strictness turned me out to where I can deal with problems and I'm ready for the real world so much more. The freedom I've had seems like the right amount. There are times when it's been cut down, but when it's over, I step back and see the situation for what it was, and the cut in freedom seems like it was helpful." He feels, however, that Pagan parents are more open to reasoning things out, instead of strict rules and regulations.

What were some things these youths might like to change in the Pagan community or in their upbringing?

Rainbow was clear: "I'd like to see them become more public and embrace other theories and other religions more. I feel there's a bit of separatism, as if other people should all come to us. Instead we should go out and join with others—not to convert, but to work together, to try not to be so separate. We should go into inner cities and get more cultures involved. We have almost no people of color: we're all white and American."

Rainbow was also tired of the "flakiness," and of the poverty that seems to accompany alternate lifestyles, feeling it reduces our credibility in the straight world. She simultaneously criticizes the "New Age" movement for being too caught up in the values of money and prestige, and missing the point of real spirituality and connecting with the Earth as something real and tangible that needs our support and attention. Clearly, what is called for is a balance between misplaced materiality and debilitating self-sacrifice.

Lasara felt that there is a deep need for improvement in interpersonal communication within the Pagan community, and feels her current and future work will focus around that. "When I am working on creating a training for people, such as 'Mindful Action,' which is nonviolence, I focus it more on self-realization and personal choice, active listening, and the tools of communication and transformation." She would also like to see more dialogue between men and women about the issues of sexuality.

She did feel that she would repeat the home schooling with her own children when the time came. "I don't think there is a school system that would teach my children what I think they need to know, or the way that I think they need to learn it. A lot of that has to do with the self-initiation aspect of it, the aspect of individuality. It's important to teach both magic and mental stuff, because we live in both worlds. I would hope I could cover all the bases."

Rainbow, who is now studying anthropology in a California university, plans to switch majors, feeling anthropology is a poor career choice unless one has the right contacts. Instead, like Zack, she wants to work with animals. "I really love the anthropology, but I love animals even more. It's fun to play with fossil hominids, but it's more fun to play with what's alive." She would like to work with endangered species and animals in captivity.

Zack feels that Pagans are basically doing things right. "Proud to Be Pagan has become my signature, and is on every one of my editorials. I think we are turning out exceptional children, with a strong global consciousness, and that's exactly what this world needs right now."

Modern Paganism is still relatively young. Only a few sets of parents have been involved in it long enough to raise children from birth to adolescence. With a wider sampling, we might get more difference in views. Yet it is clear, from the strong and articulate statements emanating from these remarkable young adults, that our first "harvest" is a good one. The crop of youth emerging in the world today will put the shallowness of their culture to shame and hopefully bring about the changes in thinking and behavior so crucially necessary at this time. Let us embrace and support them, for they are the foundation of our future.

NOTES

[1]*How About Magic*, P.O. Box 1542, Ukiah, California 95482. Subscriptions $7 annually ($8 Canada/$9 Europe), published quarterly.

[2]Mercer, Joyce. *Behind the Mask of Adolescent Satanism*. (Minneapolis: Deaconness Press, 1991), iii.

[3]Darling, Zack. "Youth and Maiden Lovemaking." *How About Magic* 1:4, 10.

ABOUT THE AUTHOR

Psychotherapist, bodyworker, Pagan priestess, visual artist, musician, writer, Anodea Judith is also past president and high priestess of the Church of All Worlds, America's oldest incorporated Pagan body. She founded Lifeways, a school for the study of healing and magical arts.

In the 1970s Anodea Judith left psychology for a time to study art on the West Coast, where she painted environmental murals for a number of years. Realizing that health and consciousness were vital ingredients in artistic expression, she began to study yoga and medication, which led to her writing *Wheels of Life: A User's Guide to the Chakra System.* During the 10 years she worked on the book, she also studied acupressure, bioenergetics, gestalt therapy, radical psychiatry, shamanism, ritual magic, psychic reading, and healing. Four of these years were spent living in the woods, engaging in magical training, vision quest, meditation, and the continuing development of the Church of All Worlds sanctuary in Northern California. Working with the magickal elements—earth, water, air, fire—in a direct and primal way gave her much of the insight into the metaphysical pattern described by the chakras. Working with clients over a 10-year period gave her knowledge of how this pattern works through human lives and its implication in healing, diagnosis, and cultural transformation.

Anodea Judith feels deeply concerned about our world's state in terms of ecology, ethics, politics, and religion. Feeling that transformation occurs simultaneously on an individual and a cultural level, she supports empowerment and balance through the teaching of life-affirming paths of wisdom, achieved through reclaiming our bodies and minds, the environment, and our connection to the Goddesses and Gods of both Heaven and Earth.

Photo © 1993 Malcolm Brenner / Eyes Open

Other People's Kids

Working with the Underaged Seeker

by Judy Harrow

The best thing anybody interested in Wicca can do—at any age—is to find a competent and ethical coven and learn the Old Ways to his or her heart's content. In a sane world, it would be that simple. But when the seeker is a legal minor or a financially dependent student, things can get complicated. Most youthful seekers come from non-Pagan families and when and if they reveal their interest in Wicca, some of their parents panic.

It is human enough to want to pass a beloved heritage on to one's children and to feel rejected when a child makes a different choice. In such cases, some parents will fear for the child's immortal soul. Others, incited by the cult-scare industry and sensational journalism, will have more practical kinds of fears. It takes extraordinary wisdom and maturity for parents to realize that their near-adult children are not extensions of themselves. Hopefully, normal parents will be able to tolerate the disappointment of a child's choosing the

Wiccan path and allow him or her freedom of religion. More fearful or bigoted parents may become vindictive or repressive.

This human desire to pass on a heritage commands our compassion as Pagans—but not our compliance. No human being has the right to control the spiritual life of another. If you are a coven leader or other Pagan teacher, and the child of bigoted parents comes to you for training, you will find yourself caught between principle and self-preservation. While in principle you should be upholding freedom of spiritual choice, you may have to walk carefully to avoid trouble for yourself—and for the young person involved.

For example, to invite anyone under 18 to a skyclad circle is to risk a charge of "impairing the morals of a minor." Even if your circle is robed, in some communities simply to offer instruction in a locally unfamiliar religion is enough to get you into trouble. It is worse for us than for the local Hare Krishna group because the average parent still believes that Witchcraft is the same thing as Satanism. As though that were not bad enough, such people do not have a clue about the difference between silly, selfish, Church of Satan strutting and the drug-crazed nihilist violence of the Charles Manson variety. No wonder they panic. If I thought some creep were leading my kid that way, I would be at least as upset as they are. So, for your own safety and for the sake of your other students, that underage kid has to wait.

And for the kid's sake. A financially dependent person is subject to all kinds of extra-legal coercion. Authoritarian parents might refuse to support their child's education unless the youngster toes the line. Some young people have been thrown out of the house before they were in any way prepared to support themselves. For a few, the risk of kidnapping and brain-washing by "deprogrammers" is still real.

On the other hand, you cannot simply send the kid away. In addition to violating your principles about religious freedom, just telling the kid to "wait" proba-bly will not work and so carries its own risk. Teen-agers' attraction to the Craft and their adolescent rebellion may combine to keep them hunting. And remember, we still have no patent on the word "Witch." Not every group that claims to be Wiccan is competent or ethical. Some groups may be sexually exploitive or use drugs or wine irresponsibly. Some have authoritarian leaders who can fully live up to the popular image of a "cult" in terms of mind control and exploitation of labor. Some practice baneful or coercive magic, bringing the inevitable psychological and karmic rebounds to participants. There are lots of ways for covens to be rotten, and slipshod practitioners are also less cautious about working with kids. Your young friend may fall prey to them.

The lucky ones will later find their ways to decent Wiccan groups, but with bad habits to be unlearned or with indelible scars. Some will experience a backlash that may carry them right into the cult-busters' propaganda machine. Others will stay with the marginal or negative groups they found, lost in a maze of dependency and despair. (The memory of one young man in particular haunts me: he never saw his18th birthday. May his next birth be into a Wiccan family that his longing may be sooner fulfilled. May we do better by the next one.)

So, if the seeker is a minor, we dare not have him in our circle. If she is an honest seeker, we dare not send her away. But, if magic is the art of changing conscious-ness in accordance with will, then there is a way out.

The waiting time can become a time of subtle growth as the seed sprouts unseen within the ground. You, the experienced magic user, can help your young friend bring flowers and fruit from the empty months.

The first thing you need to do is to present the delay as a challenge. Harness that adolescent defiance. Remind the person that it is easier and more fun to learn and experiment with the support of a group of friends, especially when one is young and unsure. Then tell him or her that solitude is a test of one's dedication. Tell about the people who for centuries kept the faith in silence or hid the Old Gods behind the images of the slave owners' saints. Ask the seeker to prove his or her loyalty by working without group support.

Second, give your friend some specific, constructive suggestions about how to prepare for formal Craft training. The experience of progress will alleviate some frustration. Your suggestions should be tailored to the individual, but here are a few examples.

Career Preparation

By definition, the underage or dependent seekers are likely to be in high school or college. Their most basic life task for now is schoolwork. Make sure that they clearly understand that we have no paid clergy, and not just because we are relatively few in numbers. As Pagans, we are creating a new kind of participatory spiritual community without the alienation that a professional clergy always creates. Preparing for adequate self-support— "right livelihood"—is a way of ensuring that when they finally can learn the Craft, it will be for love alone.

Encourage them to think seriously about choosing a career that suits their values and their talents and to study hard to prepare for it. The research, organizational skills, and habits of concentration that develop will also be useful later for Craft study and work.

Reading

Quite likely, by the time they find you, young seekers will already have discovered some of the basic Wicca reading list—such titles as Margot Adler's *Drawing Down the Moon*, Starhawk's *The Spiral Dance*, or the numerous works of Janet and Stewart Farrar. If they have not, and if they safely can be seen with such books, make sure that they do discover them. But please don't stop there.

Every young seeker should be well-informed about the progressive groups writing and working within his or her own birth tradition. In Christianity alone, consider the areas of creation spirituality, feminist theology, and liberation theology. (Some possible reading choices are listed at this chapter's end.)

If they do not really have to leave their birth tradition, perhaps they should not. Why undergo the social difficulties or lose the momentum and habits formed in childhood training, unless one must? And besides, the Wiccan community would be healthier and more stable if more people came to us because they have actively chosen the Old Ways of Earth rather than merely rebelled against some other spiritual path!

Young seekers can also use their waiting time to understand the Craft in a broader cultural perspective through learning about our sister religions, those of tribal and shamanic peoples all around the world. Later they might choose one ethnic Pagan tradition and study it in depth: its history, mythos, and practices. Besides the library, such research should lead them through the doors of museums to experience the chosen tradition's artwork and ritual objects, and to whatever relevant music and theater is available. They should take any opportunity to experience the Pagan cultures as holistically as possible. In other words, their reading should be *focused*. It should take them into accessible and relevant anthropology, history, theology, and psychology, rather than just to specifically "occult" books which are too often repetitious and superstitious drivel. If they are in college, they may be able to acquire some of this knowledge through their courses. Finally, when they come of age, they will be able to fit their Craft studies into a richer context.

Meditation

This may seem obvious to you, but not so to them. Tell them that it is the single most important thing that they can do. Meditation will bring them immediate benefits in concentration and serenity. It will help them digest and assimilate whatever else they may be learning, whether from reading or in any other way. If they are developing an art, it will be their wellspring of inspiration. Meditation can prepare them to exercise the willed imagination which is basic to most Wiccan ritual work. And it requires no props or trappings to give them away or arouse suspicion. It can even be done in a quiet corner of the school library if there is no peace at home.

Young seekers should also if at all possible keep a personal journal covering their reading, their meditation experience, their dreams, and anything else of interest. The basic theme of a personal journal is, "What does all this mean to me?" Writing things down will help them to notice and understand how different ideas and experiences are related, both to each other and to their own needs and growth. Should their parents have no respect for their privacy, suggest that they leave their journal in a school locker or other secure place. (Given that some schools conduct locker searches and that courts have not always held students' lockers to be truly private places, lockers may not always be said to be "secure.")

Artwork

If the person has any ability or leanings toward any of the arts, encourage him or her to develop it as far as possible. There are many ways to build concentration and focus, and all of them are good. Artistic expression will help the seeker to open channels for the creative and imaginative self within, which is the first and easiest way to encounter the God/dess that lives in and through each of us. What is more, the artistic skills so developed will later be applicable to ritual toolmaking or ritual performance.

Nature Study

Our religion is about the sacredness of this life on this Earth, here and now. We are "Nature worshipers," so Nature is a sacred study for us. To paraphrase, we want to see Her more clearly, love Her more dearly, and follow Her more nearly. Any ecological study, any tree and flower identification, any bird watching, or other such activities help us to understand Mother Gaia. For kids who can do so, caring for a garden is one of the best ways to attune themselves to Her cycles. Growing herbs or learning to recognize herbs growing wild is traditionally part of the Old Ways. Ecologically oriented volunteer work is a way to serve Her. Camping can be a form of vision-questing, and so can a simple walk in the park. Tell your young friend to spend as much time as possible out of doors and off the pavements with senses and heart open.

Notice that none of these activities call for candles, robes, or sigils. There is nothing about them to frighten the most paranoid parent. Better yet, not a bit of it will ever harm your friend in the slightest. There is not even a risk of wasted effort. After all, it is normal and appropriate for a kid to experiment. Young people are changeable, not fully formed. If the youngster eventually finds that Witchcraft is not his or her path after all, so what? He or she will still have a more focused mind, a means of creative expression, a greater understanding of Nature. Above all, the seeker will know what it is to pursue a goal independently, becoming a more self-directed and more balanced adult, whether a Witch or not.

Depending on the youngster's personal freedom, you may also be able to keep in touch. A person of sense and experience who can help sort out the inevitable confusions is a great blessing to any kid. Make the offer, but let the other person initiate the contacts. He or she will know when things are relatively tense or easy at home. And remember that this is an adolescent: not all issues being grappled with are spiritual. Do not offer to "mentor" unless you are prepared to help also with the general turbulence of growing up.

"Waiting is, 'til fullness." Sooner than either of you think, the time will pass. Finally financially independent and free to act on the heart's choice, your friend may will want the Craft. If so, he or she will be beautifully prepared. The knowledge, habits, and skills built during months or years of waiting will enrich ritual workings and contribute to future covens for all the many fruitful years still to come.

A Postscript

After reading this, you may wonder if there was a real person under all the theory. Actually, there were two. One 17-year-old was simply sent away by a student of mine, and he never came back. And Janet was just 16 when she somehow got hold of my telephone number. I could not bear the thought of losing another good kid. What I came up with for her on the telephone, on the fly, became the heart of what I have written above.

That was nearly five years ago. Are you wondering how it all turned out? Janet followed my suggestions for solitary study and practice, and they worked. By the time she entered college, she was well enough prepared to co-found the Pagan Student Union on her campus, effectively acting as high priestess for her fellow students, offering spiritual counsel and leading rituals.

At the end of her freshman year, she got back in touch with me. My home in New York City is a three-hour commute from her campus, but she joined our coven and has consistently attended and participated for a year now. Neither her on-and-off campus commitment to the Craft nor a normal social life has kept her off the dean's list. That academic achievement may have been what won her family over—or perhaps it was her sincerity and long perseverance. At the Full Moon in July 1991, during a family gathering, Janet's family spontaneously asked her to show them what a ritual circle was like. On her grandparents' moonlit deck, with little notice and no tools, she did. And that is not all.

On the evening of 2 August 1991 Janet was initiated into our coven. The night she first called me, had I been the kind who prays, I might have prayed for the privilege of casting the circle for her initiation. That joy was indeed mine, and there was still more, beyond my capacity to imagine or ever pray for. The next afternoon, when the coven gathered to celebrate Lúnasa, Janet's mother was with us.

SUGGESTED READING

For creation spirituality:

Fox, Matthew: *Original Blessing*. Santa Fe: Bear & Co., 1983.

Berry, Thomas. *The Dream of the Earth*. San Francisco: Sierra Club Books, 1988.

For feminist theology:

Christ, Carol, and Judith Plaslow, eds. *Womanspirit Rising*. San Francisco: Harper & Row, 1979.

Plaskow, Judith, and Carol Christ, eds. *Weaving the Visions*. San Francisco: Harper & Row, 1989.

Christian:

Ruether, Rosemary Radford. *Sexism and God-Talk*. Boston: Beacon, 1983.

Jewish:

Heschel, Susannah, ed. *On Being a Jewish Feminist*. New York: Schocken, 1983.

For liberation theology:

Cox, Harvey. *Religion in the Secular City*. New York: Simon & Schuster, 1984.

Tabb, William K., ed. *Churches in Struggle*. New York: Monthly Review Press, 1986.

ABOUT THE AUTHOR

Judy Harrow began studying Witchcraft in 1976 and was initiated as a priestess in September 1977. The study group she founded became the Proteus Coven after her Gardnerian-lineage third-degree initiation in 1980. On 30 August 1991, the members of Proteus and its 12 daughter covens in seven states formed themselves into a new, independent Craft tradition, now affiliated with the Covenant of the Goddess (CoG), a national Wiccan body.

Since then, Judy Harrow has served as first officer of the Northeast Local Council of CoG in 1983, as national first officer of CoG in 1984, and as a local and national director. She was the first CoG member legally registered as clergy in New York City after a five-year effort aided by the New York Civil Liberties Union.

A lifelong New York resident, she graduated from the Bronx High School of Science, received her B.A. from Western College for Women, and her M.S. in counseling from City College of New York. She founded the Pagan Pastoral Counseling Network and the New York Area Coven Leaders' Peer Support Group and helped create a workshop series on basic counseling skills for coven leaders.

Her articles have appeared in the *Newsletter* of the Association for Humanistic Psychology, Counseling and Values (journal of the Association for Religious and Values Issues in Counseling), *Gnosis*, and such specifically Pagan publications as *Hidden Path*, *Fireheart*, *Harvest*, and the *Covenant of the Goddess Newsletter*. For two years she produced "Reconnections," a program on WBAI-FM in New York City, on the activities of religious progressives of all faiths.

"Coming Home"

Reflections on Conversion to Wicca

by Darcie

Anthropologists traditionally define "witches" as people born with supernatural powers. As an anthropology graduate student I became convinced otherwise, taking the position that the Craft was open to anyone, that all people possess certain psychic abilities, and that Witches merely work to develop these abilities. But when I again approached the idea of "conversion" to Neopagan Witchcraft for this book, reviewing old notes and beginning a new series of interviews, I began to reconsider whether modern Witches were "born" or "made."

The majority of today's Witches were raised in seemingly "average" environments. Yet something in these children drew them towards the Craft although they had no exposure to other Witches, no words to describe their experiences, and plenty of societally approved role models to push them in other directions. (One informant even attended military school!)

Despite such barriers, these children read mythology books at an early age and researched witchcraft and comparative religions in their local libraries with the dedication of adult scholars. They collected Tarot cards and ritual tools, thinking, "I don't know quite what these things are, but I know they're important, and someday I will learn how to use them!" Many of these children had psychic experiences and received unsatisfactory explanations for the experiences when they sought help from authority. Often alone with their books and with nature, they grew to adulthood, reached out to each other, and created an entire community of individuals who had also carried inside them a secret yearning.

Many Witches explain this phenomenon by saying that if someone is a Witch in this life, he or she was a Witch or something similar (like an ancient Pagan priestess or tribal shaman) in a past life, and that if people meant to follow the Wiccan path, they will find it (or rather, it will find them). This may be why many Wiccans refer to their conversions as "coming home."

When my latest research began, I knew that the commonly held assumption was that most people "became Witches" in their early 20s. Superficially, this assumption results from the "population explosion" experienced by the Craft during the past 30 years. But it also reflects how questions are asked, for even the wording of the question itself can lead to a certain response. For instance, if I were asked, "When did you become a Witch?" I would answer, "When I was 26," because that is when I received my first-degree initiation. If I were asked, "When did you find the Craft?" I would answer, "When I was 23," because that is when I first stumbled upon and became involved in the Craft community. Yet if I were asked the question that I ultimately asked my informants, "What led you to become a Witch?" I too would hearken back to my childhood and see planted there the seeds of what I have become.

As a child, I puzzled out Greek mythology from pictures of statues of Greek gods and goddesses in my father's college textbook, *Classical Myths That Live Today.* I also studied a book of Norse myths. Before I could even read, I was quite convinced that the cherry tree in my backyard was Yggdrasil, the world tree of Norse myth, and like Odin, I spent some time hanging from its branches, gaining knowledge. Around age 5, I looked over my shoulder to see Clotho, Lachesis, and Atropos—the Three Fates. After running to my mother and clinging to her for 15 minutes or so, I was able to point out "the three women in Daddy's book" to her.

Other researchers have noted such childhood experiences. Margot Adler's comprehensive *Drawing Down the Moon* is perhaps the definitive work on the Neopagan movement's past 30 years. Adler collected stories of childhood experiences that led to Craft involvement and mentions her own: "I wrote hymns to gods and goddesses and poured libations (of water) on the grass of neighboring parks. In my deepest and most secret moments I daydreamed that I had become these beings, feeling what it would be like to be Artemis or Athena. I acted out the old myths and created new ones, in fantasy and private play. . . . I have since discovered that these experiences are common."[1]

Oberon, a Witch of "Alexandrian/Gardnerian/ Eclectic" background,[2] in his early 30s, described a similar childhood experience. An attractive, fit young man who looks more like an athlete than the library assistant he is, Oberon recalled, "I remember being so young that

I didn't have the words for it, but I was holding onto the railing of—maybe it was my crib, maybe it was just a windowsill—and I looked out the window and I could see a huge orange Moon. It was summertime, it was really warm, the sun had just set, and the Moon had just risen. It was a full Moon, this golden, orange Moon, and I had no words for what it was. I don't know if I had ever seen it before, and I wanted to—just this awe, this emotion, but I didn't have a word to say, 'Look!' or 'The Moon!' or anything, and I remember that so vividly. Obviously, you know how the Moon figures in Wicca, so that's been a real subtle influence in my whole life, just being a lunar kind of person, being drawn to the Moon, knowing when it's going to be full, or which phase it's in, without even consciously keeping track, just always noticing it. So many parts of my personality just seemed to find their home in Wicca that it was like it was made for me."

When I was a student in the Midwest, I knew a young Wiccan named Areon who was majoring in fine arts. As our friendship developed, Areon told me of childhood psychic experiences that led him to seek out the Craft. As a little boy, he often saw lights swirling above his head as he lay down to sleep. He remembered asking his mother if the lights were his "guardian angels," and she agreed. When he became older, however, he sought a deeper explanation for his visions from Catholic priests and was told that he was either under Satanic influence or lying about what he saw. This inability to get satisfactory answers from the Church led him to seek answers elsewhere, first through Masonry, then later through Wicca.

Elf Arrow is a nontraditional Witch whose mischievous eyes and fey smile betray the origin of the first half of his magical name. In an unusually serious moment for his rather sunny personality, Elf Arrow described disturbing psychic phenomena that occurred when he was a teen-ager. These occurrences led him to seek out the Craft for explanation:

"There were a lot of things that drew me to the Craft. Probably the biggest was when I was about 15. I had a couple of friends that I was hanging out with one night, and I noticed one didn't look right. It was like he was darker, and a little bit more—like he was transparent and I could almost see things behind him. And I noticed it wasn't anybody else, it was just that one person. About a week later, he died. At the time, I didn't really know what to make of that situation. I just tried to ignore it, but then it happened again with another friend. What drew me to Wicca was that I was able to find some sort of an explanation for what was going on. Before I found Wicca, I thought I was going crazy."

When Elf Arrow began to study Wicca, he learned that he was not crazy, but simply very psychically sensitive and empathic. Through Wicca, he learned techniques by which to shield himself from unwanted psychic influences.

In addition, many Wiccans found themselves drawn to magical tools as children, often not knowing what they were. When I was around 7 or 8 years old, I bought a cardboard notebook that was decorated with Tarot trumps. When the semester was over, I cut the Tarot pictures off the notebook, making them into cards. I didn't know the significance of the cards or how to use them, but I somehow felt that when I was an adult, I would find out, so I saved them. I still have and use those cards today. When as a teen-ager I was cleaning out our family basement after my father died, I came across a

black-handled, double-edged knife that had been pur-
posely dulled. I wondered why he had dulled the blade
after going to the trouble of sharpening a second edge on
the knife, which had originally been single-edged. I kept
this knife, and later discovered that it fit the perfect
description of an athame. It is my athame now.

Other Wiccans reported similar experiences. To
continue Oberon's story: "When my grandfather died,
my family inherited a lot of things you call curios, like a
crystal ball, and a five-pointed star-shaped brass candle
holder, which was a pentagram, basically. There was an
incense burner that was a little troll's head, this really
strange little thing that was not even vaguely Christian
at all, and I just collected these things and thought, 'I
don't know what to do with them now, but they're
important and I'll know someday what to do with
them, and they'll be important to me.' And sure
enough, I was right."

Laura is a 30ish Witch with serious eyes and a
cheerful smile. She works as an administrative coordinator in an important academic office, and always
includes a pentagram necklace with her office attire.
She modestly describes her job title as "a fancy word for
secretary." Laura has been involved with an Alexandrian coven for five years. As a child, she had an experience with fortune-telling cards that foreshadowed a
lifelong love for the Tarot:

"When I was young, I always had an interest in the
occult. I was very big on ghost stories, witch stories, all
that sort of stuff, which my mother thought was somewhat unhealthy, but she never censored my reading,
which was wonderful. When I was 7 years old I
obtained, somehow, a copy of the book called *Fortune
Telling by Cards*. And every child has a deck of playing

cards. I took my book and cards to school, wandered off at recess to one end of the park to just sort of flip through this book to see what was in it, and one of my friends came along and said, 'Hey, what'cha doin'?' and I said, 'I've got this neat-o book!' and showed it to her. She said, 'Oh, read my cards, read my cards!' and I said, 'But, I don't really know how,' and she said, 'But you've got the book!' So I started reading for her, and then another kid came over, then another, then another, and then the next thing I realized, the teacher was standing over me rather angrily because the entire class had sort of drifted from the playground over to me to watch what was going on.

"It was a Presbyterian school, and the teachers were not very happy: they confiscated the book and the cards. I think they called my mother and complained, but my mother just shrugged and said, 'So what's wrong with that?' which was not what they wanted to hear, but I never saw the book again, and that was that."

When Laura turned 18, she obtained a Tarot deck and resumed her study of fortune-telling by cards. She went on to read Tarot cards professionally before she became an administrative coordinator. During this period of her life she met Walter, a Witch who was to become her husband and magical partner.

Besides the psychic experiences and natural gravitation to magical tools, many Wiccans mentioned having a strong interest in religion in general when they were children. Thoth is the Craft name of a scholarly young man in his early 20s with long blond hair and a gentle manner. He is involved with an Alexandrian/ Gardnerian coven as well as an order of ceremonial magicians, and majors in both classical studies and religion at a prestigious New England university. Thoth sees his childhood interest in religion as sparking both his involvement in Wicca and his choice of profession:

"I never was a rabid Methodist. I was fortunate that when I was young, the pastor was very cool. He was the man who turned me on to studying Hinduism, Islam, and other religions when I was 9, 10, 11 years old. Growing up, that's what I read: I read books on religion and religious experience and symbols. That's what I was into. And then I considered careers in biology, literature, and then pure classical history. None of them really struck me until I found the field I'm in now, which is a combination of literature, classics, and religious studies. I'm back to doing what I enjoyed then, which is learning and comparing world religions and human experience. I think Wicca will help me in my work. I think it offers a chance to develop perceptions that are completely outside of acceptable scholastic forms. Yet the people already in the field don't even know that, necessarily, because they themselves are so limited within certain monotheistic, Judeo-Christian or Western, major, traditional frameworks of reference. And I think that Pagans can bring their own experiences, what they've gained from their beliefs, into play when examining the same material these other people are working with. I'm really looking forward to being able to be a practicing Pagan with beliefs, and study Pagans from the ancient world because a lot of the material has been misinterpreted, I feel, by Christians, Jews, or people without the Pagan mindset."

Besides mythology (usually Greek) these young Wiccans were influenced by a great variety of books. Some mentioned the predictable authors: Dion Fortune, Starhawk, Sybil Leek, Hans Holzer. Yet even something as seemingly insignificant as one of those small books sold in the grocery store checkout line was capable of having a profound impact on Oberon simply by what it symbolized.

"When I was 11 years old I was in a supermarket with my mother, and I found a little Dell Pocket Book, one of these little 25¢ things. It had a pink cover with a black cat and black candles and was called *Everyday Witchcraft*. It was by Delphine C. Lyons. I'll never forget it. It was a little book that had practical magic—love spells, how to find things. It wasn't even so much the content that was important, just that here was an adult, a responsible person, who actually had a lifestyle that somehow incorporated it. I felt something in me, an opening, or an overshadowing even, of a terrible, dark—not terrible like awful, but terrible like awesome—great dark knowledge that was in me or was there to be tapped but I somehow didn't know how to access it yet. From there it was just a matter of finding a book in a bookstore, and it would be like a bell rang and I would know, 'Oh, yes, this is the next step on my path.' It just felt right; I knew it was a path, and I was being led somewhere, and it just blossomed from there," Oberon said.

But a conversion experience, however meaningful and dramatic, is useless without follow-up. Thus I moved to the second part of my inquiry: Once Witches embrace the Craft, why do they stay with it? What lasting benefits do Witches receive?

Most Wiccans who were still new to the Craft spoke at length about personal growth and spiritual development. Tom, involved with a coven based on Celtic tradition for 20 months at this writing, spoke of the "sense of wonder" that many Wiccans refer to when describing their spiritual path:

"I still have that sense of wonder. I feel that I started on something that's very important, and I've kept with it so far. I feel more a sense of belonging. I think that was a little surprising. It usually takes me a long time to get close to certain people, but right away there was a sense of acceptance, community."

It is that sense of acceptance and community that seems to stick with Wiccans as the years go by and to become more and more important to them. While individual spiritual growth is important in Wicca, leading some of our religion's critics to label us "self-absorbed" and "self-obsessed," most Wiccans of at least ten years' standing now emphasize community service, citing a need to assist and strengthen the growing Pagan community as a motive for deepening their Craft involvement. Having "come home," they now wished to make home a place to accommodate the ever-increasing numbers of "new relations" showing up at the door.

For example, Elf Arrow has been studying Wicca for the past 12 years, most of that time as a solitary. While he didn't feel he needed the Pagan community, he came to believe that the community needed him:

"For the longest time I stayed in the Craft because I felt it helped me grow as a person. While that's still true now, a lot of what has me here too is trying to help other people. There are a lot of outside influences. There are a lot of leaders in the Craft. You have people telling others what to do. Yes, it might be kind of egotistical [for me to think so], but it's not my ideal of what I think everybody should be guided by, and I think part of my reason for staying in the Craft and part of my reason for getting involved in the community now is to help people who are just coming into it and learning to grow. I want them to view Wicca as something they find within themselves, not going to someone and saying, 'Okay, how shall I think, what shall I do?' but being able to work within."

Michael, 38, can best be described as a "high energy" person. He needs that energy because he was initiated 20 years ago into an Alexandrian-based Wiccan coven and a magickal order and is now high priest of those same two groups. He holds classes twice per week in addition to rituals, and he is concerned that so many people are now attending his groups' holiday celebrations that his household's large basement temple room can barely contain all of them. Michael spoke at length of his coven's tentative re-entry into the Wiccan community after 17 years of refraining from community involvement because of political infighting:

"The re-entry into the community is simply due to the fact that recently we've met more people, and some of our younger members have influenced us to come out of the broom closet. Some of the older members still want nothing to do with the Pagan community. They're negative to the extreme that it's almost fanatical, and it is upsetting to me. I'm glad to be re-entering the Pagan community. As long as we don't get involved in the politics, I don't care. We want to be an influence for Wicca. As we come out, we're trying to keep away from the political arguments and just say, 'Look, let's practice Wicca. Let's practice Paganism and let's have a real good time doing it.'"

Whether or not Pagandom needs paid clergy is another matter forcing more of us to speak out. Elders who have quietly run covens for years are finding that Wicca is being defined in the media by those Wiccans who are drawn to the limelight. But are good public relations skills the only thing necessary to good leadership? Does today's Wiccan leader need to be showman as well as shaman? Will the quiet, thoughtful leaders be pushed into the shadows? More Wiccans are becoming concerned with ethics than ever before. Many feel the perceived "clergy/lay split" that some Wiccans are talking about is actually a "paid clergy/unpaid clergy split," and that the voices of low-profile elders may be lost in the shuffle of a Wiccan circus.

Consequently, many Wiccans who feel that all should share equally the stresses and joys of priestesshood and priesthood are beginning to promote community service as an important part of Wiccan training. Laura's husband, Walter, a quiet man with a kind smile, is an Alexandrian-based eclectic Witch who works in a film library. He spoke to me about his ideas for Wiccan training that strongly involve community service: "The other side of the coin is the service angle, service to the community, Pagan and otherwise. This is why we started Conjure Cinema.[3] I have felt for a long time that if you were going to proclaim yourself as a priest or a priestess, then that is a service role and you need to take that aspect of it seriously.

"When my wife and I first joined a group, one of the first things that they did, after reading our questionnaires and a few book reports, and getting a general feeling for us, was to tell us what they felt we needed to work on. They told me I needed to work on compassion, that they didn't think I was a very compassionate person. They decided that in order to correct this I was to do volunteer work at a hospital in order to learn how to be compassionate and how to see those less fortunate than myself.

"I said, 'You've got to be kidding. I'm compassionate. I don't kick old ladies. I feed scraps to stray dogs, whatever.' But they said, 'No, no, that's not what we're talking about. You go do this.' So I went to Glover Hospital in Needham, Massachusetts, on Saturday mornings, and I grumbled the whole time, 'I don't believe I'm having to do this. I'm X number of years old, and here I am having to change bedpans and drag breakfast around to these old people.' Well, that was my compassion speaking! I did it for about six months, and it did what it was supposed to do. It got the point across to me, and I was rather glad that I did it. It taught me not only about compassion, but about the need for service, not just to our community, but to the community at large. If you're going to call yourself a priest or a priestess, then you need to know what that means. It doesn't mean a matter of personal power, of 'Here I am invoking these god forces: I grow the horns and the bushy tail, power, power, power.' That's the furthest thing it means to me. It means that you go back and look— just go back and look at your regular church, what the priests supposedly are doing there: food drives, clothing drives ... I'd like to bring the idea of service back into Wicca."

Yet even an experienced, service-minded Witch like Walter still benefits from the tremendous personal spiritual experiences the Craft has to offer. As our conversation progressed, Walter went on to describe his year-long reign as his coven's Harvest Lord. As Harvest Lord he experienced an intense communion with nature unlike anything he had ever felt before:

"Last year I went through our coven's Provider Cycle as Harvest Lord, and that was an astounding experience. It was very, very different from anything else I'd ever gone through, and it was an incredible year, and also a very terrifying year for me in that I'd read *Harvest Home* (a novel by Thomas Tryon) and I knew it was based on that, we would do the cycle of the seasons.

"I enjoyed the first ritual, the Awakening, but about two days afterwards I started getting this very odd feeling. I've always liked to hike, and just be out in the open. I like going out to the fells to hike around, but this time when I went there, I felt very different. I felt that the trees were sort of bending to be closer to me, the wind was rustling more my way, and it was sort of spooky. It was like the trees were bending, almost bowing in front of me to acknowledge me as Harvest Lord. I started to get a little freaked out by it, and I thought, 'Well, I'd better go talk to my coven about this,' so I did, and they said it was perfectly normal. As I explained it later, it was like living that whole year in an hourglass where I was completely suffused in that energy. Sometimes you get energy like that in ritual if you've done a very good ritual and brought up a cone of power. You may get this real—for lack of a better phrase—'energy high,' which lasts until you've burned it up at the end of the ritual. Well, it was like living in that state for the entire year. I would really feel the lives of the trees and the grass, anywhere I looked. If it was something natural, it was calling to me all year long.

"That was great until autumn because I knew about the story's ritual, symbolic killing at the end, and I decided I could accept it. Then one day I was sitting on a bench, reading a book, and this one, lone leaf came down out of a tree and plopped right next to me on the bench, and I've never been more terrified. It just boggled me how scared I was; it was just like a signal saying, 'Your time, your time, it's coming!' It was the same thing as in the spring when the leaves and the wind were all very nice and very grateful to me. Now all the dead leaves would go out of their way to float down into my path and say, 'Reminder, T minus 60 days.' I didn't think I was going to last until the ritual because even though it was symbolic now, I could very much understand the mindset of people who had gone through the cycle for seven years of prosperity. Just going through it for one year, I had an amazing feeling of being caught up in it all that year. As I approached the ritual, there was a small feeling of fear, but there was also a feeling of exultation, of wanting to rush forward, about wanting to greet it with open arms to say, 'Let's do it, let's get it over with!'

"By the time it came time for our Harvest Home ritual, I felt, 'Yes, yes, get that sickle out, rush me on that blade!' But I was very scared on that final day. I was scared not of the symbolic death, but of going back to just being myself. I didn't want to let go of the experience because it was so unlike anything that I'd ever felt. I wanted just to hold onto it and keep it with me. I didn't want to go back to being plain old myself after that. So we went through the ritual; I had the symbolic death, and the instant the sickle touched my throat, everything just went 'Whoosh!' out of me, all my exultation, all my fears, all my worries, all my concerns, gone, just gone. I fell over and BAM! hit the floor, and that was it. I did a temple sleep that night, saying goodbye, saying thank you."

Such intense experience provides a form of spiritual nourishment that keeps Witches like Walter from burning out on too much service

If, therefore, Pagan conversion is not usually an unexpected, dramatic occurrence but rather is experienced as a compelling force driving one through life, it would be difficult for a Wiccan who experiences such a force to leave the Craft. One of my informants, Oberon, attempted to leave the Craft when he moved away from his coven to another state. He had made the decision to commit to a relationship, and decided to put the Craft on a shelf while devoting all his energies toward making that relationship a success.

He found, however, that the Craft would not be ignored; it called to him in subtle, yet compelling ways: "I've had gaps where I didn't go to festival because I'd got involved with someone who lived in Rhode Island, and I moved down there. It was difficult to come up here [Boston] for a Saturday night and be able to make it back to Rhode Island. Just because of where my head was at at the time, my frame of mind, I lost my involvement in it, not wanting to. I put more importance on the relationship, and I came to discover it's not good to submerge your own interests for someone else's, so it started invading my dreams. I would dream of being out on a moonlit night, and I'd feel this tremendous but subtle energy pervading my life that sought expression like the magma in a volcano. It wasn't violent like that, but it did seek its expression, so I finally started going back. I knew I had to. Once I started going back, things were fine. Everyone in the group was still just as close and the spirit was still there. So I started going back to sabbats, and our Tuesday and Thursday night rituals. Eventually I moved back from Rhode Island and now I'm back living with my coven."

Since many Wiccans cite childhood experiences as leading them to Wicca, one would think that the majority would be in favor of Craft involvement and initiation at a very young age. Yet actually the opposite is the case, and many feel initiation is appropriate only for adults. Sometimes this is because Wiccans felt they were "railroaded" towards their parents' religion when they were children; other times it is just because they feel that youth should be a time of exploration and not commitment. Elf Arrow comments on this:

"I guess my feeling is that I hate to see anybody get involved in the community right off the bat. My first choice is the same road I went, where a person first does a little bit of personal study and develops his or her own ideas. The problem with coming in green off the street, so to speak, is that you can bump into anybody who claims to be an authority and have them tell you what to do, and then you're right back in Catholicism—there are no moral decisions to make. 'Look at this book: just follow this line by line and you're all set.' There's no free thinking to it, no trying to decide if what you're doing is the right thing or not, and I think that people who walk into the Craft green have a chance of bumping into someone who may lead them astray, or may just lead them to beliefs that might not be right for them. My suggestion to teen-agers who are interested in the Craft is to study on their own and come back when they can answer that moral question themselves, when they can decide whether they should follow this path, even if their parents disagree with them, and they're ready to start studying with other people. Until then, that's not a decision someone should make."

Since Michael has been a high priest of a Wiccan coven and magickal order which has existed for almost 20 years, I asked him how he has handled the issue of underage participants:

"From just the way I was trained by my teacher, anyone under the age of 18 would have to have both parents' permission before we would even let them come to our house. Legally, it's too much of a danger for us to even consider. If we had both parents' permission, we would consider it. We've never had it happen, because most of the people we find have come to college originally or come to Boston on their own somehow. Because Wicca is a Pagan religion, it is a fertility cult. We specifically do not worship skyclad [nude] all the time, but it is a matter of choice, so in the summer when it does reach very high-level temperatures, most people go skyclad, and there is a question of legalities, of contributing to the delinquency of a minor and such, if a parent decides to complain. Sexually, of course it's no problem, and it's never been a problem in the group because we don't include sex as part of our worship; it's an individual thing. It's part of the religion in that it is a religion of life, but we do not make it part of our religious worship. It shouldn't be a problem, but of course it would be viewed that way whether we did it or not by someone who would question us because we were going skyclad around someone who's young. It would be very difficult for us to have to deal with that, and there is no reason why we should have to. Anyway, people under the age of 18 probably don't know what they're looking for completely yet anyway. It's a questioning time period. In that case, we'd give them study, we'd help them in any way we can, but we'd wait until they were 18 before initiation." (For additional information on this issue, see "Other People's Kids," pp. 93–103.)

In *The Hundredth Monkey*, Ken Keyes, Jr., describes a concept which may explain why so many people seem to be drawn to the Craft at this time and why the Craft has taken root in the lives of so many children whose seedling Craft experiences seemingly received no outside reinforcement or support until they reached adulthood. Keyes asserts the idea that "when a certain critical number [of people] achieves an awareness, this new awareness may be communicated from mind to mind"[4] through the collective consciousness.

It may be that awareness of the presence of and need for the Goddess reached such a "saturation point" some 25 to 30 years ago and has been spreading through the collective consciousness ever since. This could explain experiences such as that described in a letter I received from a 19-year-old college freshman in Vermont:

"I'm Wiccan, but I 'came home' fairly recently. For years before that I had held secret goals of re-starting a faith which worshiped the Goddess—little did I know it was already there!" It is also possible that the revival of Wicca is just one manifestation of a greater environmental awareness currently spreading throughout the collective consciousness.

This may also explain why Wicca appeals to a broad spectrum of people, regardless of religious background. In *Drawing Down the Moon,* Adler includes the results of a questionnaire by religious scholar J. Gordon Melton, and a similar survey of her own regarding the religious backgrounds of today's Pagans.[5] These studies tested the popular notion that most Pagans are former Catholics and Anglicans, drawn to the Craft because they enjoy religious ritual. Both studies actually found that the religious backgrounds of today's Pagans mirror the composition of American society, with the exception that the percentage of Jews is doubled. This finding did not surprise me since as a former Lutheran I have always been drawn to aspects of the Craft other than ritual. It would be interesting to see the results of a survey on the backgrounds of self-confessed "ritual junkies," for whom ritual is indeed "the big draw." Perhaps the Catholics and Anglicans will show up here. It would also be interesting to study exactly which elements of their religious upbringing Pagans tend to keep and adapt to the Craft, why Jews are doubly represented, and if the growing popularity of CUUPS (Covenant of Unitarian Universalist Pagans) is increasing the representation of Unitarians.

Looking ahead, our children may have quite a different experience of Wicca than we do. Many of them will grow up immersed in a pre-existing Pagan community. With our community's explosive growth and the efforts to establish Wicca as a legitimate religion alongside the so-called "great traditions" (Christianity, Judaism, Islam, Buddhism, and so forth), our children will not have to wait until they are legal adults to enter the community and feel like they have finally "come home."(See "Between the Worlds," pp. 75–91, for some of these young people's responses.) Will they "stay home"? Or will they leave Wicca, not feeling the call, and pull of it the way the current generation did, and so "leave home." If Wiccan retention mimics that of other religions, one will leave for every three that remain.

Yet even now some Pagan parents are reporting that their children show signs of spontaneous, Craft-oriented inspiration. Recently on the Boston public-access cable television program "Real Witches," folksinger Tzipora Klein (of the former duo "Kenny & Tzipora") mentioned her daughter Maeghan's desire to stop the family van so that she could get out and see the Moon, saying, "It just doesn't seem right to see Her through glass right now." Tzipora went on to say that some Craft and folk traditions prohibit viewing certain phases of the Moon through glass—information that Maeghan had not been formally taught at the time.

Furthermore, the idea that most Witches are born, not made, can be seen to support non-traditional self-initiates' desire to be considered fully fledged Witches outside of any initiatory lineage. Yet most of my informants came from such lineages. Does this idea indicate that people unable to recall childhood "signs and omens" should not become Witches? If they really want to become Witches, such exclusion would be cruel and totally out of keeping with the spirit of the Craft and of the Goddess as Great Mother.

Instead, I prefer to think that there is a little bit of Witch in everyone and that everyone has the potential to hear the Craft's call. Perhaps that is why some people fear and hate us so much: they fear the small, hidden part of themselves that wishes desperately to abandon the strait-laced confines of the mundane world to follow the music of Pan's pipes to Arcadia, where they would truly "come home." One thing is for certain: the Craft will continue to call, and its call will be answered.

NOTES

[1] Margot Adler. *Drawing Down the Moon: Witches, Druids, Goddess-Worshipers, and Other Pagans in America Today* (Boston: Beacon Press, 1986), 15

[2] "Gardnerian" refers to the initiatory lineage associated with the English Witch Gerald Gardner (1884–1964), co-creator of much of the modern Craft. "Alexandrian" refers to the lineage of Alex Sanders (died 1988), ultimately derived from Gardner's. Many modern Witches also describe themselves as "eclectic," meaning outside any one tradition but borrowing from any.

[3] Walter shows movies and videotapes at his home every month. Movie goers are asked to donate food, clothing, or books for the homeless. Donations are made in the name of the Pagan Assistance Network (PAN).

[4] Ken Keyes Jr. *The Hundredth Monkey* (Coos Bay, Oregon: Vision Books, 1989), 17.

[5] Adler, 444.

ABOUT THE AUTHOR

Born in Chicago on the Ides of March in 1961, Darcie received her B.A. in anthropology from Purdue University in 1982 and M.A. in cultural anthropology from Northern Illinois University in 1986. She has written for Pagan magazines since 1985, her work appearing in *Harvest, Rainbow City Express, New Moon Musings,* and the Covenant of the Goddess newsletter. She is best known for her column, "Darcie's Current Events," which ran in the now-discontinued Pagan magazine *Harvest* for several years.

Trained in the Alexandrian tradition of Wicca, she received her second degree in 1987 and holds ministerial credentials through the Covenant of the Goddess.

She is one of three co-producers of "Real Witches," a public-access television program cablecast in Boston.

Her interests include her niece Deirdre, poetry slams, and support for Pagan prisoners.

For public lectures and video presentations, write to Darcie at P.O. Box 15230, Kenmore Station, Boston, Massachusetts 02215.

Initiation by Ordeal

Military Service as a Passage into Adulthood

by Judy Harrow

Buds sleep in winter. As the sun slowly returns, they gradually swell. Then, one sudden, surprising morning, we find every tree on the street covered with tiny, tender leaves. Human growth is like that: seasons of gradual change punctuated by moments of sudden breakthrough. This is how Tony remembers his experience on the "confidence course" during Air Force Basic Training:

"The obstacle is called the 'weaver.' Two telephone poles are set at a 30–degree angle to the ground, connected by tie bars about every three feet. You go sideways over the first bar and under the second, then continue alternating till you reach the top, about seven feet off the ground, and drop off.

"I found it impossible at first. My back muscles just weren't toned for the reverse push-up movement it required. I dropped off after the third tie. The training instructor told me to start again. I dropped off a second time.

"He had me stand at attention while he yelled at me. He said he didn't believe I had actually tried. He said that I could do it if I let myself get angry enough. If I couldn't, he said, he'd send me home to my momma. And then, he told me that I could drop off, if I wanted, at the red tie bar, about 2/3 of the way up, where the women recruits would drop off. The concession was what really did make me angry. I started again

"I realized halfway through that I was actually doing it. When I reached the red tie, the instructor asked if I wanted to get off. I shouted 'No, sir!' and went to the top.

"Later I was astonished—astonished that I had done it at all, and that I had refused his offer of an easy out. Astonished that muscles I never knew I had could hurt so much. And, yet, now I knew they were there, and I knew I could use them again at need without a training instructor there to goad me on. Years later, the knowledge stays with me, literally ingrained into my body as well as my mind."

These days, we postpone marriage and vocation long past the advent of adolescence. The old puberty rites may still change us from children to youths, but not to grownups. Folk wisdom says joining the Army will "make a man of you." And so for some young men— and young women—military service makes and marks the delayed passage from youth to adulthood.

Here's a classic description of initiation into adulthood: "The term 'initiation' in the most general sense denotes a body of rites and oral teachings whose purpose is to produce a decisive alteration in the . . . status of the person to be initiated. . . . To gain the right to be admitted among adults, the adolescent has to pass through a series of initiatory ordeals; it is by virtue of these rites, and of the revelations that they entail, that he will be recognized as a responsible member of the society. . . . In philosophical terms, initiation is equivalent to a basic change in existential condition; the novice emerges from his ordeal endowed with a totally different being from that which he possessed before his initiation; he has become another. . . ."[1]

Eight Pagan military veterans shared their memories and reflections with me. I am grateful for their frankness and generosity. All eight had enlisted voluntarily. Their enlistment dates range from 1952 through 1987. Two were in the Army, two in the Navy, three in the Air Force, and one in the Marines. Two saw combat. All have now returned to civilian life. Two intend to re-enlist; one has refused to accept his veteran's benefits. But all, even he, believe that their military experience moved them into adulthood.

They enlisted for a variety of reasons. Bob quit high school to enter the Marines as an escape from his dysfunctional family. Paul, as a youngster, had been fascinated by his stepfather's dog tags, hanging on the bedpost. Phyllis was looking to "get out of the nest and see the world."

Fritz said, "I finished high school in 1956. I knew better than to do what other people of my economic class in my hometown did, which was just get a job in the mill. Most of the young fellows who had gotten those jobs were already missing fingers. It was a miserable existence. The only way I knew that a poor person could get out of my dismal town was to join the military, so I did. I joined the Air Force."

As Ben told it, "I joined the Navy in 1979 as a hard-hat diver. I was 23. I went into the military because of a combination of blind and irrational hormones and just dealing with the day-to-days of a working-class kid trying to cut academia and pay the bills. It just got to a point that I felt a need for some kind of adventure."

For Paul, "Something wasn't right in my life. Finally, I decided to go check out the recruiting officer. We talked and we talked. He suggested that I wait for an opening in some technical specialty. But the nearest one was about nine months away on a delayed entry program. I didn't want to wait that long. In my life, I needed the change. So, in 1987 I signed up for infantry against everybody's advice, including the recruiter's."

In retrospect, some can identify deeper needs and motivations. Fritz reflected, "I was in the grips of what I now recognize as the need for an initiatory experience. I intuitively knew that unless there was something life-threatening or some small risk, even, of life-threatening activity, it wouldn't count. Now, you may ask why I didn't accept the challenge of working in the steel mills or coal mines, which was certainly life-threatening enough—and it was because there was no element of heroism in it, no adventure."

Paul, one of few who already knew he was Pagan at the time of his enlistment, recalled, "I always worshiped a hunter-gatherer God, and so I saw no problem going into the military and being a Pagan. Most of my Pagan friends were highly anti-military. My priestess at the time tried to talk me out of it, but my priest was more supportive."

Departures

Rites of passage often consist of three major phases: separation, transformation and re-integration.[2] Looking closely, we could see Basic Training as a passage in itself, an initiation into military life. The duration and intensity of military Basic Training, and its underlying structure, are similar to traditional, tribal initiations. Or step back a bit, and look at the several years a youngster will spend in the military as an extended initiation into adult life. In that view, Basic Training can be understood as a very strong method of separation. Sharply and suddenly the young recruit leaves behind all that was familiar.

Ex-servicemen and women report indelible and poignant memories of leaving home, leaving family, and of their first moments of contact. Paul: "I got up early on the day I left for training. I tried to wake my brother up to say good-bye. He barely woke, said, 'Yeah, good-bye,' and went right back to sleep. That was kind of disheartening. Then I left. I remember waiting for the bus, feeling so alone for the first time in my life. Like I was finally, totally on my own. It was an odd feeling, like a step into manhood."

Brett: "My Dad dropped me off at the Academy, and that was it. I was alone in the middle of the drill field with my suitcase. Since that day, I've never taken any support from my parents. It was just very much a setting free. That in itself was a rite of passage, of being on your own, because you can't go back."

Phyllis: "They make sure that you arrive in Texas in the dark, at night, tired. So they've got you right there. They've disoriented you completely. They've got you exhausted and they've got you in the dark. And then they start yelling at you almost immediately. You know: you will do this and won't do that. They just take you right over."

That shocking first contact, like the traditional "Guardian at the Gateway," serves as the first challenge to the neophyte. Bob: "I joined the Marines to see if I could do it. I got off the bus and I said, 'I made a mistake.' I knew I had got myself in over my head. I still had to prove to myself that I could do it. I lasted it. It was seventeen weeks of Hell."

Basic Training—Separation from Childhood

"During their time of separation from the community, the initiates experienced a ritual death and rebirth. Boys passed away and men emerged. In order to evoke the virtues of courage and strength, this transition involved ordeals of danger and self-denial. In psychological terms, the ordeal served to evoke the archetype of the hero . . ."[3]

Basic Training normally includes intense physical fitness training, instruction in military terminology and etiquette, training in the use of weapons, and more. But it is not just like going to any trade school. All instruction is presented in the context of powerful psychological techniques that are also part of classical initiation processes around the world. At the core of Basic Training lies intense, carefully delivered, psychological stress.

Training instructors deliberately use humiliation and verbal abuse. Fritz: "It was really a big surprise. I had the idea that the service would treat us in some sort of chivalric fashion. I was very surprised at how rude and rough they were with us, how mean they felt it necessary to treat us."

Phyllis: "Eventually, you get to know a routine and you know what is expected of you, so it's not as disorienting. But it can be just as frightening, because they won't give you any inch. They try to keep you a little bit off balance the whole time." A series of confusing, apparently irrational demands adds to the stress level. At the Merchant Marine Academy, Brett recalls, plebes walking the building corridors are required to stop and do a "face turn" at every corner.

With behavior so strictly controlled, eventually every recruit is caught making mistakes. Punishments increase the pressure. They do not simply humiliate. They are also designed specifically to deprive the recruit of recreation and of sleep. Brett: "At the Academy, your day was planned so that you got up at 5 a.m. and got to bed at 10 or 10:30 p.m., so you'd always be tired. There was never enough time to do everything you had to do by way of shining your shoes, your buckles, your buttons, your pins, etc., to be ready for inspections. So, it would be 10:30 at night, after lights out, and you'd get out the flashlight and start shining your shoes.

"To add to the pressure, they would give you extra duty for things that seemed inane and trivial. Once, I had to guard the head (bathroom), several days in a row, with my rifle. I had to challenge everybody that entered to identify himself as 'friend,' 'foe,' or 'Communist subversive cockroach.' This was during time that the rest of the section had free to do whatever they wanted."

Paul: "They had me on a lot of extra duties. I was doing fire guard in the middle of the night every single night. On a seven-hour night, I had to get up for a two-hour shift in the middle of the night, every night except Sunday. And I also had to do extra details in the platoon, plus I had to maintain my own stuff. So, I wasn't getting enough rest, which created more problems because I fell asleep sometimes when I shouldn't have. I lost every single day pass that came up."

Peer pressure, too, was deliberately engendered. Bob: "They would pit you against other people. If someone was overweight, for example, it was up to us to whip them into shape. They would turn us against each other. They'd say, 'I'm coming back in five minutes, and if he doesn't have this done by then, you're all going to get it.' One time somebody didn't take a shower, and a group of guys jumped this guy and scrubbed him down with scrub brushes."

Phyllis: "When you had somebody who wasn't quite pulling it together, everybody suffered. If one girl screwed up, you all got your privileges taken away, or you all got jumped on. So you all kind of made sure everybody else was toeing the mark. And you became responsible for one another, which you might not do as a young person out doing a job. You learn that you're affecting other people's lives."

Training instructors do not actually hate young recruits. Their exaggerated hostility, ridicule, and anger are a role assigned to them by the training model. Eventually, most recruits see through the act, and this gnosis removes much of the sting. Fritz: "The drill instructors used a lot of psychological violence against us. It took me a couple of weeks to pick up on the fact that their hearts really weren't in it. Most of them didn't believe it would work. They would occasionally just walk away from an encounter, disgusted, I think, with themselves. And, after a while, they just gave it up. I think the whole thing might have been an act."

Brett: "They put you under severe stress, and they don't let you realize at the time that it's all false. It's all fake. There's nothing real there, really. I mean there's no real threats, but they seem like real threats to you at the time. They do it so that, when you are presented with a real threat, a real stress situation, you won't break."

After Basic—Assessing the Changes

Basic is tough. But those who complete it are not just glad it's over. They report a rueful kind of pride, a firm basis for bonding, and greater confidence in their own strength and capability. Paul: "You get proud of it, and you laugh at it afterwards, because you do get by. And they do let up after a while, but you've got to earn that."

Brett: "Because I went through all that crap, now I can deal with almost anything. Right now, I'm under a lot of stress in my life. When my wife left me, I only missed one day of work. I was broken up and everything, but by the second day, I was able to pull myself together enough to go to work and do the bare minimum requirements of my job. I wasn't excelling at it, like I usually do, but I was functional. It's because of my military background that I was able to do that."

Paul: "They want to get you to the point where you will crack, and then cut it off there. They don't want you to crack. They want to push you to your limits to make you harder and stronger, more able to take it. They don't want to push you past that point."

Bob: "What I still have is the camaraderie and the bonding. Whoever made it, we can say we've been through that, we can go through anything together. You know going into any situation that somebody who can handle things is watching your back."

Phyllis: "We all knew that we'd all gone through it, and we could relate to each other at least on that level. You know, we were all terrified and we were all thrown off. We were all screamed at, treated like morons, generally humiliated. When you got done, you know that, if you could get through that without going crazy, you could handle anything. You also knew that the people around you had that same kind of stamina."

Ben: "Basic Training hardened me physically and also in a lot of terms mentally. Along with the physical conditioning goes a technique of resolve that where you can't quit, you won't quit. There is no response except success, and no excuses. How to deal with a stark reality, and making rapid choices, in an instant, a split second."

Brett: "After going through the artificial stress at the Academy, I went to sea. Whether it was on merchant ships or when I was on active duty with the Navy, there were always things that you had to decide that could be somebody's life depending upon it. On an oil tanker: who's going to go out on deck and close the tops of the tanks that you've been washing when you get into heavy weather. Who's going to do what with which lines when you're docking. There are some dangerous jobs that if a line parts, the guy's dead.

"A lot of the things that people find stressful in business life, somebody that's been through a military experience isn't going to find stressful. People come screaming into my office now, saying something or other is an emergency. I sit there relatively calmly. It frustrates them to no end. I say, 'What's the emergency?' They say, 'We could lose half a million dollars if this computer doesn't start working in the next ten seconds.' I just go about my business, and they want to know how I can do that. But there's nothing there that's that important, no emergency, no one's life depends on anything. You know, it's only money. What is money?"

Ben: "In my teens and my early twenties, I was the lost youth, that confused, James Dean-kind of figure. I was given a focus. Still to this day, when I need to sit down and focus, I can do it. I can sit down and deal with a problem for twelve hours at a time if necessary."

Paul: "I learned something else in the military which carries over to civilian life. I always accomplish my task, my mission. I may leave other things by the side doing it. But, for example, at work, I do things that nobody else can get done. I will get the job done, period. Sometimes we get too many orders in and my boss starts to panic. I say 'don't worry, I've never not gotten it done.' He always leaves me alone to do it, finally, and I always get it done."

Fritz: "The other thing that I noticed years later, when I moved to Canada and became a back-to-the-land hippie, was that you could sure tell which guys had been in the service and which guys hadn't just by looking at their woodpiles. It wasn't just that it was tidy; it was big."

I used to be opposed to conscription on simple political grounds. Listening to the veterans, I came to understand the gritty reality of their experience. I became convinced that military service is a valid initiatory path. Now, as priestess and counselor, I am appalled that anyone was ever forced into it. Such a path should only be undertaken by free and careful choice. And, as with any valid path, one who has willingly begun should not easily be diverted.

Ambrose: "In the military, you cannot leave if you don't like something. So, you are forced to go through the experience. As you know, life itself does this. That, I think, is valuable."

The veterans I spoke with are all Pagans, all used to thinking in terms of ritual. Most agree that in Basic they experienced a true initiation.

Phyllis: "Basic is definitely a rite of passage. You either make it or you don't. In the real world you might not take having somebody get right up in your face and scream at you, but there you've got to, or you know you can be sent right back to day one and start all over again. They'll put you through it and put you through it, until you get it."

Ambrose: "Military Basic Training rids people of false timidity. I think a lot of the timidity of people is not real: it's a habit or something that's a presumption on their part. They're not really that timid, but they don't know it because they haven't experienced yet the things that they're shying away from. Once they do, a lot of that falls away, and they become no longer timid, but careful."

Brett: "It's the difference between being a child and a man, almost immediately. If you're not a man by the time you report in, you're certainly a man by the time you're done with Basic Training. Actually, it's an experience that I think everybody should go through. I had a lot of hell at the Academy, but it's an experience that I would not give up for anything."

Fritz, although he appreciates what he learned in the Air Force, had to wait a few more years for his true initiation: "Basic definitely did not make me a man. It made me more clever and conniving. It taught me to keep my head down. It made me lose my respect for the people in authority. All those things are valuable, but I don't think they contributed to my manliness."

Non-Combatant Assignments— a Day Job in a Uniform

Even during a war, only a minority will actually participate in combat. Most perform support services. Phyllis was an aircraft mechanic in Germany: "You go to work and you come home. That's it. You work your shift. While you're at work, you do your job. When you get off, off comes the uniform, and you're on your own."

The Air Force trained twice as many radar technicians as it needed in 1957, so Fritz painted signs in Portland, Oregon, and lived as a civilian: "I had a room in the barracks, which I never slept in. I stayed with friends downtown in their college-type communal houses. I'd come back out to the base on the bus every morning, take a shower, eat breakfast, go to work in my uniform, leave work, eat supper, take the bus into town, and hang out, party, study. I started taking college courses in the evenings. I just put in a very minimum effort in the service for my remaining two years."

Simple enough, but there was no active combat during those years. Others that I spoke to had noncombatant assignments during wartimes, while friends from training were in danger. Safety, in such circumstances, was not at all comfortable. Ambrose: "I wanted to fight, and I was trained for it. But I didn't actually go to Korea. I was in Seattle, at Pier 91, boarding the ship. I was probably halfway up the gangplank. I remember it struck me so. Somebody came around with a clipboard. Fifty names out of the five thousand of us were being taken out and reassigned. I was one. I was given a different assignment, on this continent.

"I was very pissed. I didn't like it at all. My adrenaline was up. I was packed and dressed and well into it. I was really prepared, prepared to take a wound if necessary. I was all dressed up for the party and the party was canceled. The disappointment lasted a couple of years.

"My second reaction came when I heard of the first person that I knew personally that was killed. I wondered why I wasn't there. I wanted to know if I had any personal responsibility there. Did I do anything at all to not go when I should have gone? That's what I had to clear up."

Bob: "I was never in combat. People that I trained with died in Vietnam. I felt I should have been there, with my friends. The Marines did nothing to help me handle my guilty feelings about not being there.

"I felt bad until just a few years ago when I met another Marine veteran in a bar. He told me it was not my fault. I had followed orders. It's not like I copped out and got myself ordered to Guam, so I'd be safe. But I still have the feeling like I should have been there to help my friends."

Combat—the Warrior's Initiation

All proper initiations force us to face critical issues in our lives, to make choices and commitments, to set our course for the next period of slow and incremental growth. But just as not all people are the same, neither are all initiations. Different issues are presented along different initiatory paths. The military initiation, besides being a general initiation into adulthood, is a specific initiation into the way of the Warrior. Those who enter the military must face, directly or indirectly, the question of violence. All know that they may be ordered into combat at any time. All are trained in combat skills.

Ambrose: "What they learn about violence is going to have to be supplemented a bit, because they don't learn the morals of violence. They learn courage and accuracy. They learn how to operate in violence."

Draft boards used to frequently hit applicants for Conscientious Objector status with this hypothetical question: you are walking down the street with your aged, infirm grandmother. A gang of muggers approaches. Would you defend her? If you say you will, your application for CO status will be denied. By current legal standards, whoever would defend their elderly grandmother is required to kill without question anyone the government points them at. Pagan ethics point to a very different kind of standard.

"If it harm none, do what you will," says the Wiccan Rede, the core ethical statement of our religion. A few of us interpret the Rede as an absolute, a mandate for Gandhi-style pacifism. Other Pagans may avoid all military participation because the high-tech nature of modern warfare is ecologically devastating, intolerable even to those Nature worshipers who would, at need, draw sword.

For others, the Rede is a statement of situational ethics. The grandmother/mugger hypothetical demonstrates that in real life absolute harmlessness is often impossible. That realization relativizes the Rede.

If muggers attack your grandmother, somebody is going to be harmed. Belief that you are absolutely forbidden to harm the muggers may impel you to let the mugging take place unhindered. Your passivity could harm your grandmother emotionally at least as much as their aggression harms her physically. In such a situation, you can only choose whom you will harm. Still you are responsible, as always, for the outcomes of your choices. The Rede provides no guidance, but natural loyalty does, and so does a normal sense of justice.

We can also set beside the Rede our heritage of Warrior God/desses and hero myths from almost all Pagan cultures. These model fair and honorable combat. They teach us that we have the right and obligation to defend ourselves, our communities, our sacred ways and, most of all, our sacred Earth.

Bob: "I want to know how to kill so I can protect myself and my loved ones. I don't want to assault, I want to defend. Everybody should know how to defend themselves and their loved ones. The important thing for a true Warrior is not knowing how to use the sword, but knowing when to use the sword."

Contemporary Paganism, drawing on many sources, supports what has been called a "high-choice" ethic. A statement by the First Officers of Covenant of the Goddess made during the 1991 Gulf War reads in part: "It is CoG's policy to support individual matters of conscience. We understand that devotion to the Goddess may either direct individual members to participate in war, or to conscientiously object to participating in a war. We pray that the wisdom of the Goddess guide all members of our faith who face such a decision."[4]

So, conscientious Pagans handle the question of violence just as we handle any other truly important issue. We find out as much as we can about any given situation, apply our values as well as we can, choose on a case-by-case basis, and accept the consequences of our choices. In legal terms, this is called the "selective Conscientious Objector" position, and it is not recognized as a valid legal option. The "all-or-nothing" standard of the draft laws infringes on Pagan religious teachings, which insist on our right and responsibility to choose. By so doing, it also violates the American Constitution and the freedom the American military purports to defend.

Paradoxically, whoever chooses to enter the military by that very decision chooses to give up most other choices during his or her term of enlistment.

Ben: "Discipline is everything. It ain't *Star Trek*, where they talk about motivation or initiative. The first and last issue is discipline for an enlisted man. You're told to do something, and you're expected to perform."

For Pagan youth, trained to a high-choice ethic, the military emphasis on taking orders will be especially challenging. But when you have chosen of your own free will to fight for a cause you truly believe is just, your moment-to-moment actions need to be coordinated with the rest of the team. Proper coordination both maximizes effectiveness and minimizes risk.

Furthermore, total obedience during the initiatory period is another classic characteristic of tribal initiations. "Between instructors and neophytes, there is often complete authority and complete submission. . . . The authority of the elders is not based on legal sanctions; it is, in a sense, the personification of the self-evident authority of tradition. . . . The passivity of neophytes to their instructors, their malleability, which is increased by submission to ordeal, their reduction to a uniform condition, are signs of the process whereby they are ground down to be fashioned anew and endowed with additional powers to cope with their new station in life. . . ."[5]

Military obedience does carry that initiatory quality. Bob: "We were constantly being told what to do. You were never allowed to think for yourself. There was never a choice. It was part of trying to break you down mentally. Once they have you broken down and pliable, then they make you into who they want you to be. They want you to do what they tell you without stopping to think about it."

Ambrose: "But this discovery makes you a more limber and more adaptable person. When your pride gets battered, it turns you in on yourself in—I think— valuable ways, and brings out a maturity. The ability to take orders, even from someone that you feel is stupid, is valuable. It loosens up unnecessary stiffness in the personality. When you resist, that's when you hurt. Pain comes from resistance."

Phyllis: "You have to have a certain amount of willingness to bend. But, it taught me some things about myself and about other people that were good."

Historically, recruits enlisted in the military for "the duration" of a particular conflict. They committed themselves to causes they knew they could, with good conscience, support. But modern weapons technology requires far longer periods of training. An army can no longer be called up, trained, and fielded within a few weeks. Now, people enlist for a period of years, not knowing what conflicts may arise during their term. The military emphasis on obedience to orders remains necessarily unchanged in this changing circumstance.

Ambrose: "The point of military training is not the particular weapon that you're using at the time; the point is that you use it when you're told to."

The idea of battle, of glory, carries a certain romantic allure. Paul, whose assignment was noncombatant, holds this dream: "War is like nothing else in the world. You change, you transform by the idea of war. There is nothing else like it on the face of the world. Not martial arts training, not the Guardian Angels, nothing. From those, you go home at night. This is your life, twenty four hours a day. And you accept it and thrive on it. You become a soldier, a Warrior, a servant of the people."

For some, it really is like that. Ambrose: "I was in South America as a mercenary soldier. I thought it was a just cause, and so I went. I still think that it was a freedom fight.

"Combat causes things that nothing else does. It's the shock of dealing with somebody that wants to kill you and the realization that you're going to have to kill them in order to live. I can't describe what that does to one very well.

"The intensity of the teamwork. Not the camaraderie, but the teamwork itself. Gung ho, in Mandarin Chinese, means working together, and that's what it is. You learn gung ho at high intensity when your life is at stake. That brings people to their maximum efficiency. The violence, the facing of death, the baptism of fire. That's what's unavailable anywhere else, and I'm glad I had that."

Others felt the same intensity of focus, the same quality of teamwork, but remember these as evil seductions. Ben: "Down south, I had to deal with killing people. It was that wonderful word, an 'insertion.' That's what a short-term conflict is called: the team is inserted into a situation. When you think about it, it's like a rape.

"We were mining a harbor . . . and we ended up hitting a couple of little bases there to make sure everything was going to go smoothly for the mining vessels . . . and we hit a refinery . . . and from what we could tell at the time and from what I suspect looking back, I think we took out a village at the same time. I think that's what really flipped me out.

"Even while I was there, I was having dreams of my grandfather saying, 'What in the hell are you doing, man?'

"But there's this kind of trance-like state in motion that you exist in, and you just follow it through until you come to the end. The one issue with all these specialty teams is 'no excuses, no retreat, you do it.' Very much like Thor, it's all or nothing. You don't even question it, because you have been programmed. There's a kind of a wild cross between joy and aggression. As a natural adrenaline rush, it's incomparable. It's about as hard as a methamphetamine rush.

"Your team goes through training together, so by the time you get out of UDT school, you are set up in your team structures. That team is very much like a pack of African wild dogs. There's a commitment to the group. No matter what, you're committed to help. If somebody's a little behind, you pull them through. You do it.

"So, I managed to get through it. But the time comes when you get off the adrenaline drive. And then—I just couldn't handle it. I went into this really heavy guilt reaction. I spent the five days coming back on a ship just in a ball. I kept coming back to what had I done? What is this? Why is this? What am I doing here? This no longer is where I'm coming from. The adventure's over. This is the adventure: blood on my hands. Like Lady Macbeth, I was trying to wash the blood from my hands. It can never be done.

"I have destroyed everything I ever had from them. As far as I am concerned, I am not a vet. I was a thing. And I wish nothing to do with it. I have refused my veteran's benefits."

Only one thing distinguishes Ben's account from Ambrose's. Ambrose believes he fought in a just cause. Ben does not. And the only opinion that counts for this purpose is their own. Certainly, orders must be given and taken for any combat team to survive and prevail. And yet, we remain responsible for the consequences of our acts. A Pagan ethic still requires autonomy and personal responsibility. As many of these veterans see it, these also constitute the honor that distinguishes the soldier from the Warrior.

Ambrose: "To teach people to kill people they don't know, on the orders of someone else they don't know, in a place they have never seen before—this thing is alien from the Warrior. The Warrior does not fight for other people. The Warrior does not kill strangers unless the strangers are invading. The Warrior does not fight for national interest in other lands. The Warrior does not go to a war because he's told to go to a war."

After his term in the Air Force, Fritz actively opposed the American invasion of Vietnam. He draws a distinction: "I have never been against war. I was against that war. I never had anything against the Warrior archetype or Warrior energy. I now know that I was striving very hard to manifest archetypal Warrior energy. I sought it out in the service. I couldn't find it there. So I went and found it somewhere else.

"I have tried always to manifest the Warrior's line-drawing capacity, the ability to say, 'That's okay, and this isn't okay. It's okay to go to war against Hitler, but it's not okay to go to war against the people of Vietnam.' Draw the line and say, 'This far and no further.' Call that anti-war or anti-military if you want, but it's certainly not anti-Warrior."

As polytheists, we understand that, just as there are many ways to be Divine, there are many ways to be human. For some of us, the Warrior archetype stays in the background, lending a certain quality of boldness and determination to whatever it is we do. Others see themselves primarily as Warriors. This is their lifetime calling, their spiritual path.

Ambrose: "By the time I was 12, there were a couple of things that I knew to be true. One is that there is a war and I am a Warrior. I knew I was on that Path. It wasn't the war people around me were talking about. It wasn't World War Two. It wasn't 'the war within.' I didn't know what war it was. And I knew I am an artist—mine is a double Path. And I knew the Supreme Being to be female, and the planet to be a live being. And I felt a bond to the Earth and into the past.

"I have learned that my real war is the war against evil, or the war against some agent of evil that's responsible for the killing of this planet. It can be won, I think."

Re-entry—The Failed Phase

Step back again, a moment, and look at the whole term of military enlistment as a classic, three-phase initiatory experience. The first part, Basic Training, elegantly accomplishes the separation from adolescence, carrying the new recruit to the limen, the threshold at which transformation can happen. Combat training and for some the experience of combat give the neophyte an intense experience of aggression and violence. The young person discovers and defines her or his relationship with the Warrior aspect. This self-confrontation very effectively fulfills the transformation phase.

But the third phase of initiation is to return the candidate, changed, to the community, to occupy new roles and receive new status based on the new wisdom that initiatory changes have created. Only with re-integration is the initiatory process complete. And this is the moment at which the military fails. In contrast to the intense weeks of Basic, there is maybe a day, maybe two, to do paperwork and return equipment. Then, with no psychological preparation and no demarcatory ritual, the new adult civilian is back home. Each has to work out his or her own re-adjustment and re-integration, usually without guidance or support. It's never easy, and it's not always successful.

When we fail to bring our warriors back into the civilian community, we place them—and ourselves—at serious risk.

"Those who become warriors must of necessity assume a changed psychological state in order to kill the enemy and win victory. . . . After battle, the community may recognize th e need to return the warrior to a new role and identity in the culture. The warrior identity must be transformed into a new identity that demands maturity and responsibility. Failure to achieve this transformation of the warrior identity may lead to alienation and the assumption of a victimized state . . ."[6]

Brett felt a loss of focus when he returned to a less structured civilian environment: "The hardest thing for me to deal with was deciding what am I going to wear? I was used to a set routine, at the Academy or on ship. I didn't have that routine anymore. Without it, without knowing what I was going to wear, and stuff like that, I've become somewhat slack in certain aspects of my life.

"I've gotten slack about the way I keep my home. If I kept my quarters at the Academy or on ship the way I keep my home—forget it! I've also gotten somewhat slack in the way I take care of myself, my body. I used to keep myself in better physical shape, exercise in some form every day.

"Some of it is that there are just so many more things that can catch my eye. I tend to spread myself thinner than I did previously. I was going through life with a bigger set of blinders."

Phyllis went all the way back home again. Faced with the old expectations and the old reinforcers, her newer self eroded: "For a while I was changed. I had more confidence in myself. No one could tell me that I couldn't do something. People couldn't act up around me. For instance, my sister and I drove cross-country with some friends. The husband and wife started to fight out in the middle of nowhere. I just got out and said, 'Now, everybody knock it off. You shut up and get in the back, and you get in the front. I'm driving.' I took charge of the situation. My sister said she didn't know it was me.

"I'm more reserved now. I wouldn't jump into an argument between a husband and wife now. I'm not sure why I lost that. I wish I hadn't. Perhaps it was because when I got out, I went back into my parents' home. I fell back into the whole pattern of being the dutiful youngest daughter. I also went right back to my old job. I had taken a military leave of absence. When you come back, they have to give you your old job back. It was like going back to square one. It might not have been a very good idea, but that's what I did.

"I think I can probably get it back if I thought real hard on it."

Paul made a premature ritual gesture of separation, and lost what was for him as a child an important symbol of adulthood: "I let my priestess convince me to chuck my dog tags. I was having real trouble integrating back into civilian life. She suggested, 'If you really want to make a break, do a symbolic magickal thing. Chuck it off of the back of the Staten Island ferry, like leaving it behind you.' I've always regretted that. I've only myself to blame for listening to her." Similarly, Tony, all alone in his new apartment, put one of his uniforms into the dumpster as an intentional symbolic statement.

A slick return to *status quo ante* did not work, and neither did a superficial gesture of separation. The transition out of military life is every bit as complex and demanding as the transition into it. The absence of any structure for making the shift makes it much harder to work through the process, but in no way lessens the need to do so. It is hard, but it can be done. It has been done.

Fritz: "When I came out of the service, I was a fire-breathing enthusiast for the military and all it stood for. Fortunately, I had some friends. One of them suggested that I go spend the winter on a Quaker communal farm in Canada. This was my real debriefing. They were all pacifists there, and they were real eager to talk with me about my military experience.

"That's when I started getting into psychological trouble. I could see that the military wasn't the solution to the world's problems, because it was hopelessly fucked up. But I thought some sort of physical power was necessary to straighten the world out. What these people did was put me on the path that it might be some sort of spiritual power that was necessary to do the job that I knew needed to be done.

"When I left there, I started my actual journey. I went around the West looking for work. I ended up in Los Angeles just in time for the world's first Peace March on Easter Day in 1961. I went from there to Berkeley, where I got recruited to go on the Freedom Ride.

"I'd learned in the military to go out and get what I wanted on my own. The military wasn't going to give it to me, but it did teach me that I could do it, myself, and so I did it. I went to Mississippi. I went to prison. I went around all the places in the South doing voter registration. I was actually for the first time being effective in a life-threatening situation, what I'd been looking for from the beginning.

"That summer of 1961 was a noticeable rite of passage. All of a sudden, I was grounded. I was rooted. It was like I had a tattoo on my forehead that said 'initi-ated.' I became a person that had lots and lots of friends and lots of things to do and lots of wonderful adven-tures. I was no longer adventureless. I no longer had to make my own adventures. I was welcomed into the society of people who were having adventures.

"That's what I wanted out of the service. I think I got it because what I learned in the service was that's not where to go for it, and I can get it myself, and here's how to do it. I came out of the service self-propelled. I came out of jail in Mississippi an initiated person, ready to go to war, which I did.

"My revolution got under way in '61, and caught fire in '63 at Berkeley. That was the year of the Free Speech Movement and all that sort of stuff. My original involvement with the movement against the Vietnam war was street theater: demonstrations in Berkeley and at the draft board in Oakland. Later, I moved up to Mendocino. There we got in touch with some Methodists who were moving draft resistors up to Canada. I helped with that for a couple of years.

"It truly took a Warrior's self-discipline to choose to stay out of the military, and to make all the moves that were necessary to get your ass to Canada. A lot of the people who set their foot on that path didn't con-tinue because they lacked Warrior energy."

It is hard, but it can be done. Even under the most challenging of circumstances, it has been done.

Ben: "The military expects you to perform. And they give you all the training you need to perform. But when your term is up, they don't deprogram you. When you're dumped out, that's part of the problem. You get all this really weird, nasty shit that just goes through your system. Someone just may trigger it, and you lash out. Just like a wild dog.

"It got so at least I learned not to go to bars. I'd rub up against some working-class character and there'd be a scuffle, and people would be hurt. Who needs all the hot water and the chats with the cops? In recon, special forces, UDT, the Seals, two-thirds of the guys that go through it come out psychically wounded.

"I went back to school, spent two years failing as a human being there, feeling un-human, or like a troglodyte or something. Isolated and not clean—spiritually just filthy. I realized I couldn't go on. I was tired of not being around people, having people not want me to be around. What am I going to do about this? Am I going to go through it all my life, or is there something I can do about it?

"You could talk about some kind of shamanistic experience where that person was left behind. You can use the image of the snake shedding its skin. This shedding of skin took five or six years. I kind of walked into being somebody else. I feel much better every day now. It's probably still ongoing. Only recently now I want some bits and pieces back from the warrior that I was before.

"I got into the Navy because it was a great lovely game. I think a lot of people all had the same mindset. We make absolutely horrible, terrible mistakes in our lives. That's what this was. And then, here we are. This is where it's at. You're in crisis, and you've got to turn it around. Either the lever's going to break or the rock's going to move. I guess I was lucky—the rock moved.

"In a lot of ways, you're just a kid until you get to a decision like this in life. And then, here's your initiation to adulthood. I may find out as I go through all this that what happened to me back then may have just been a key crisis in my life where I was forced to make a decision on my humanity. Can I just go through life sliding and not making a decision?"

We are the civilian religious community to which Pagan veterans return with their initiations often so painfully incomplete. Our job starts here. We can and should provide spiritual counseling and ritual services to mark the process of reintegration. As Paul's experience shows, this cannot be a one-shot ritual, no matter how beautifully designed. Rather, we need to organize peer support groups, perhaps facilitated by elder veteran peer-counselors, in which veterans can face and work through their bad memories, assess and celebrate their learning and growth, and assist each other to re-learn civilian lifeways. Following the Native American model, larger rituals should mark when such a group begins and ends its work. This demonstrates to veterans that their families, covens and community respect them and support their efforts.

They will not be returning to us unchanged—to expect they would is foolish and destructive. For our own benefit as well as theirs, this needs to be recognized with new roles and status for returning veterans. Those who have learned that their life lies along the Warrior path are already in places taking on the role of providing security at our gatherings. Others may use their new-learned ability to function under stress as public spokespersons. Many will want to advise younger people about what the military experience might mean for them.

Many of us are not veterans, but still want to help. The advice the veterans give us about how best to be helpful is simple and common sense. Don't rush them. Don't pry. Listen. Don't judge. Whatever they did, you've never walked in those shoes.

Ben: "They have to do it in their time, and not in anybody else's. Just be absolutely supportive. They're going to go through a lot of stuff. You can't stop anybody from doing anything, but just stand by them. Give them a lot of room. If they're feeling dirty, all you can do is just wait for them to open. Make sure everybody in the community is there to catch them when they fall."

Ambrose: "When they come back, don't ask them what they did. Don't ask them what it was like. Let them talk, be prepared to listen, but don't probe. Let them pace it."

Ben: "Make it absolutely clear that, whatever has happened, that they're okay, that they're part of the community. They're a good person, even if they've gone through all this.

"You look at the Vietnam experiences. The guys were already coming back guilty. Telling them that they're a rotten dirty shit just doesn't help either. Then they're not even accepted back into their communities, and then they're lost. You see so many of them lost and on the street."

Informed Consent—How Shall We Advise the Young?

Some of you reading this may be thinking about entering the military. What advice would I give you? Others may be parents of teenagers, or relating to teens as priest/esses, teachers, elder friends. What advice would we offer them? I don't believe we can just tell them "go," or "don't go." As Pagans, we believe that the choice and the responsibility rests with them. And if we have raised them well, to be autonomous and self-responsible, they wouldn't listen. As trusted elders, all we can do is to guide them through a decision-making process. It starts with being sure they have a realistic picture of what to expect.

Ben, on the basis of his civilian skills, was promised assignment as a diving instructor. After his name was on the line, his assignment was changed. He says: "When somebody is contemplating the decision, be completely honest with them. Recruiters are never going to tell you the whole truth because they are in need. So they're going to paint a very rosy picture of the situation.

"Make sure they know that whatever is put on that paper isn't worth the stuff that comes off the round tube beside the toilet. An enlisted man is nothing but a piece of meat. They own your ass. They really own your ass, no ifs, ands, or buts about it. If you're willing to accept that, okay. You have no power, absolutely none."

After the reality check comes the ethical check. When this country had a draft, those who sought Conscientious Objector status were required to write an essay defining the religious and philosophical reasons for which they declined to participate in the military. That was a fair requirement, as far as it went. The problem was that it carried a built-in assumption that whoever could not give a good reason against it would enter the military.

But joining the military is not trivial. All who do will undergo a severe and serious initiatory process. Some will later be commanded to kill or die on somebody else's say-so. Wouldn't it be wiser to ask all youngsters, regardless of whether they do or do not enlist, to write an essay outlining the pros and cons, and giving the reasons for their choice?

Writing such an essay, clarifying their thoughts and feelings, would also be, for all of them, a step into maturity.

Ambrose: "In primitive society, the young are not presented with a choice about initiations or rites of passage. In our society, the decision is a phase. It is part of the initiation."

From a Pagan standpoint, what they finally decide is far less important than that the decision be made with full knowledge and full consideration. Fritz: "Life's a dance. Your dance may take you to Canada, or to a grave in the sand. It may also take you to the war and safely back. You have a lot of choice about what your dance is, but don't make any moves without thinking them over real carefully. Sometimes, if you're going to be a Warrior, the right thing to do is to go to war. And sometimes, if you're going to be a Warrior, the right thing to do is to stay away from a war. The best way to find out is to find out as much as you can about the war, because all wars are not the same. Go do your dance, but do it mindfully."

Ambrose: "If anyone were asking me what should they do, and they're 17, I would recommend the military training experience without a war. However, there is that risk. There hasn't been a war since World War Two that in my opinion was right, that anyone should have gone in. And I see nothing coming up either. There's no threat to this country from another country."

Because modern military enlistment is for a term of years, I believe all potential recruits who take responsibility for their choices and actions ought to research current world affairs and American foreign policy. There's still a lot of disagreement about various recent incursions, so let's use the genocidal Indian Wars of the last century to demonstrate that our country is not morally infallible. Pagans, who do not give oath lightly,

need to look before they leap. Although no one can pre-
dict events perfectly, recruits should be satisfied that in
any reasonably predictable conflict, the American military will fight on the side that they feel is just.

The risk of being caught between your conscience
and your given oath can be minimized, but it can never
be completely eliminated. Fritz: "Almost anything
worthwhile requires some sort of time commitment and
some sort of release of authority to an Other. This may be
a real initiator or a false initiator. There's almost no way
to tell except through the experience. So signing up for a
military term, knowing full well that during that period
you may be ordered to do something against your conscience, is entering a potentially initiating situation."

Ben's story, like so many others, shows that killing
people in violation of your own conscience puts your
very sanity and soul at risk. This is the final, awful, possibility that faces every member of the military. No
young person should enlist without at least acknowledging this risk, and considering what his or her
response might be.

Let the last word come from Ambrose: "If I were
talking to a person, I would begin with what the military does for them, and see whether they could get that
anywhere else these days. If they could find it somewhere else, they should. It's a prickly decision."

Taken at face value, that sounds like an anti-military statement. But I say much the same thing to young
seekers after Wiccan initiation. "Don't do this unless
you have to." It's the advice of initiates to seekers on all
Paths, in all lands, at all times.

SUGGESTIONS FOR FURTHER READING

On Initiation

Eliade, Mircea. *Rites and Symbols of Initiation: The Mysteries of Birth and Rebirth.* New York: Harper, 1958.

Mahdi, Louise Carus, Steven Foster, and Meredith Little, eds. *Betwixt and Between: Patterns of Masculine and Feminine Initiation.* LaSalle, Illinois: Open Court, 1987.

Raphael, Ray. *The Men from the Boys: Rites of Passage in Male America.* Lincoln, Nebraska: University of Nebraska Press, 1988.

On the Warrior Archetype

Bly, Robert. *Iron John: A Book About Men.* New York: Addison-Wesley, 1990.

de Vries, Jan. *Heroic Song and Heroic Legend.* Oxford: Oxford University Press, 1963.

Gilmore, David D. *Manhood in the Making: Cultural Concepts of Masculinity.* New Haven: Yale University Press, 1990.

Moore, Robert, and Douglas Gilette. *King Warrior Magician Lover: Rediscovering the Archetypes of the Mature Masculine.* San Francisco: Harper, 1990.

Pearson, Carol S. *Awakening the Heroes Within.* San Francisco: Harper, 1991.

On Return to Civilian Life

Imber-Black, Evan, Janine Roberts, and Richard Whiting, eds. *Rituals in Families and Family Therapy.* New York: Norton, 1988 (especially Section 1: "Defining and

Designing Rituals")

Krippner, Stanley, and Benjamin Colodzin. "Multi-Cultural Methods of Treating Vietnam Veterans with Post-Traumatic Stress Disorder." *International Journal of Psychosomatics* 36 (1989): 79-85.

Metzer, Deena. "Re-Vamping the World: On the Rebirth of the Holy Prostitute" in Zweig, Connie, ed. *To Be a Woman: The Birth of the Conscious Feminine.* Los Angeles: Tarcher, 1990.

Wilson, John P. *Trauma, Transformation, and Healing: An Integrative Approach to Theory, Research, and Post-Traumatic Therapy.* New York: Brunner-Mazel,1989.

(Special thanks to Fred Lerner—"Fred the librarian"—for helping me find many of these resources and for every much else—JH)

NOTES

[1]Mircea Eliade, *Rites and Symbols of Initiation,* (New York: Harper & Row, 1975), x.

[2]Victor Turner, "Betwixt and Between: The Liminal Period in Rites of Passage" in Louise Carus Mahdi, Steven Foster, and Meredith Little, eds. *Betwixt & Between: Patterns of Masculine and Feminine Initiation,* (LaSalle, Illinois: Open Court, 1987), 5.

[3]Fred R. Gustafson, "Fathers, Sons and Brotherhood" in Mahdi, et al., 170.

[4]*Covenant of the Goddess Newsletter,* 16:2, (Imbolc, 1991).

[5]Turner, 9-11.

[6]John P. Wilson, "Culture and Trauma: The Sacred Pipe Revisited," in John P. Wilson, *Trauma, Transformation, and Healing* (New York: Brunner–Mazel, 1989), 42.

Photo © 1993 Malcolm Brenner / Eyes Open

Handfasting

Marriage and the Modern Pagan

by Jeff Charboneau-Harrison

What is marriage? It's the reunion of the separated duad. Originally you were one. You are now two in the world, but recognition of the spiritual identity is what marriage is.[1]

Comprehending marriage in the modern age is a significant question for Pagan and non-Pagan alike. It has been said that marriage is an outmoded institution and that marriage is just too difficult to carry through. Hopefully, in the Pagan world, love, power, and magick can still be gained through handfasting, for in the larger society, we find near indifference to the marital union's spiritual significance.

Marriage can be one of the most significant rituals we take part in, for it will have a lifelong effect on every level of our psyches. But today we seem to have lost consciousness of what marriage is or could be about. By binding ourselves together in such a union, we are able to place two souls into a transformational cocoon from which both can emerge with wings. But these ideas are lost, for today there is much uncertainty about relationships in general. There are no more clear-cut rules and guidelines to follow when it comes to a couple's romantic interaction. Of course this new freedom is overdue and welcome, yet now more than ever it is up to the individuals involved in a relationship to determine the meaning behind their connection. Many couples have responded to this lack of guidelines by living together without a marriage ritual, yet this does not solve the problem: the same challenges exist within a union whether or not it is officially recognized.

We have all seen today's divorce statistics and have witnessed, if not been involved in ourselves, marriages that just do not work. Moreover, even if we do find partners to whom we are especially well-suited, there is always the fear that things will change and that the conditions appropriate for spiritual growth might not be the same in a year or two or ten. This fear is well-founded, for in any relationship—romantic or business—change is a given. The challenge is to lay a strong spiritual foundation at the onset so that change will bring growth without chaos.

Pagans partially address this problem by having two ceremonies, "The Year and a Day" and the karmically binding "Eternal Rite," but even so, these ceremonies' meanings need to be considered more closely. The Year and a Day rite is actually a trial run to see if the couple wants to enter into an Eternal Union. This chapter will address the more permanent ritual, for it is the ceremony that acknowledges a couple's spiritual identity.

As Pagans we are aware that within the larger culture spiritual significance has gone out the window in practically every area of life. Rites of passage, rites of death, in fact any major marker of life's significance—including marriage—pass with little commemoration of the inner reality lying behind the outward form. Often the ritual itself seems to be more of a nuisance than anything: the couple just wants "it" to be official. Vows have crumbled into hollow utterings while the couple's kiss only lets us know that the "ceremony" is over.

This one-dimensionality is why many of today's Pagans were yesterday's Christians; it means it is up to us to create ritual that embodies our beliefs and to define for ourselves what marriage means. As Pagans we are still products of the larger culture, and perhaps we have unconsciously adopted our society's superficial views of marriage. In the larger culture, wedlock has become not much more than a state-approved economic and social arrangement that includes the right to have sex. Yet there must be more than an economic arrangement, sexual convenience, and a social sanction to this sacred interchange. The marriage of souls is what it is all about: a connection that will allow the most rewarding and fulfilling recognition of Self for both partners. Both the handfasting rite and the marriage relationship should be built on the spiritual drama that is occurring between the partners: this is the wellspring from which all other aspects of the relationship flow.

Throughout the ages there have been many reasons for marriage besides love. Families arranged marriage between their offspring for power and wealth, as did individuals. Such relationships may achieve their mundane objectives, but ultimately the people involved become disillusioned and disappointed unless the union develops love.

A spiritual marriage includes all aspects of love, for in order to unfold the partners' spiritual drama, deep love must be present. Love means an *opening* of one person to another—allowing another human into yourself. "Love is an act of consciousness and means opening one's own limits of awareness to that which one loves in order to become one with it. This has happened only one when has taken into his own all which represents the partner."[2] In the East it is said that love is surrender, and here we are talking of surrendering the boundaries we place between ourselves and others. Fears that we cannot be loved, fears of being hurt or of loving too much are walls that block love's flow. Once our fears are dismantled, we are freed to find love and are then allowed to discover the spiritual connection that should be the focus of the union.

Defining love's nature is an entirely different matter, for love is the most complex of emotions. The term "love" covers not only romantic relationships but those between parents and children, between friends, between siblings, and between master and pet. The difference seems to be that romantic love involves a yearning and need for one's partner. Humans need intimacy and physical connection with other people: these "illogical," instinctive feelings can escalate to the point that a person thinks he or she cannot exist without the lover.

Sexuality is the mystery at work here, and sex is important to a romantic relationship. Pagans know the connection between sexuality and the divine. We realize that a sexual relationship's energies transcend us as individuals. Feelings of sexual attraction and need can be pleasurable and exciting, but a sexual connection does not necessarily indicate that a karmic, spiritual relationship exists. For that reason, Pagans have the option of the "Year and a Day" handfasting.

During that year and a day, the couple can cool down from their initial sexual attraction (just a little, in some cases) in order to better judge their spiritual connection. I am not saying that sexuality is not "spiritual," only that the physical connection between two souls should be seen as a sacrament and not the relationship's main focus. Sexual interplay mirrors the spiritual: "As above, so below" *and* "As below, so above." The language of lovemaking can express the interplay occurring on all levels of the relationship, yet the physical sacrament of sex must be used as a gateway to other levels.

On the spiritual level, we must understand first and foremost that in marriage we sacrifice our individual egos to something larger than ourselves. This does not mean constantly giving in to what one's partner desires but instead to what is good for the marriage itself. By enacting this principle the partners truly become part of the One that is greater than either of them alone. The Yin-Yang or T'ai Chi figure symbolizes this idea, for each partner circles, flows, dances, and reacts to every move and nuance of the other within the circle of wholeness— indeed, Oneness. In his book *The Power of Myth*, Joseph Campbell states that our inability to grasp this concept is one reason marriage has become so precarious today.

> I would say that if marriage isn't a first priority in your life, you're not married. The marriage means the two that are one, the two become one flesh . . . if you are acquiescing constantly to it instead of to individual personal whim, you come to realize that that is true—the two really are one.[3]

Acquiescing to a marriage does not mean losing one's individual spiritual destiny. On the contrary, it means recognizing an individual's true relationship to the realm of spirit, for it signifies the recognition that the One is not just the individual but the two partners together.

Realizing a couple's spiritual identity points us towards the *hieros gamos* or Sacred Marriage of the Goddess and the God. The Pagan Wheel of the Year celebrates various stages of the *hieros gamos* from the courtship of the God and Goddess in the spring to the Divine Child's birth at Yule. All are of great importance to us in our discussion of marriage.

In ritual, the *hieros gamos* can be seen obviously in the physical consummation or sacrament at the end of a handfasting ceremony. At this time the bride takes in and expresses the Goddess. She becomes All-Woman in response to her groom, who has become the powerful and virile God—in other words, the All-Man. Several things are occurring. The handfasted couple has become the Divine Couple so that they are directly manifesting pure God and Goddess energies. On the physical level there is also the alchemical mixing of the male and female sexual fluids. This elixir is the actual physical substance manifesting the God and Goddess energies. By partaking in this exchange, the couple creates a spiraling helix of male and female, God and Goddess energy, so that the male may partake of the female element and the female of the male element. In this process each person is allowed to become whole: the two have created something greater, and from this union the Divine Child is conceived. The Divine Child is the *marriage itself,* the two that are one. Of course, the *hieros gamos* should not only occur at the handfasting but throughout the couple's life together.

This reunion of the male and female polarity is not only part of the *hieros gamos* but an everyday part of the husband and wife's interaction. Males seek to express their inner female *(anima)* and females to express their inner male *(animus)* in order to become whole. But sexual polarity is not the only aspect of spiritual discovery that unfolds in a strong union. The marital partner acts as a mirror to any undiscovered, unknown, repressed, or unrealized aspects of ourselves. This region of the Self has been called the Shadow, but Shadow does not mean bad or evil, but means rather beyond our *conscious* recognition. It is the alter ego or the other half of the whole. The Shadow may include a man's unrealized femininity or a woman's unrealized masculinity, if these parts of the Self have not been integrated into our conscious interaction with the world. Edwin Steinbrecher, in his work *The Inner Guide Meditation*, described formalized relationships like marriage as "Shadow-dancing":

> The unconscious interaction between the two people involved produced psychic and physical movements which to me seem like dancing—each having to respond or react quickly to the projection coming from the other when they are in the same physical space, each taking as perfectly as possible the unconscious role needs of the other.[4]

Each partner lives out all that the other does not know or accept about themselves, positive or negative. This is where the recognition of spiritual identity we have been discussing comes in. For example, your wife's incredible artistic ability is also yours, but you have yet found this trait in yourself. By observing her and understanding her expression of this energy you may come to recognize that you also have such talents. Often we see in relationships that one of the partners is the "quiet" or "passive" one and the other the "talkative" or "dominant" one. Whatever the polarity may be, the goal is for both partners to integrate and transform themselves as individuals.

Unfortunately, the same realizations apply to negative traits. You must take responsibility if your partner acts in a negative way, for he or she is mirroring something back to you. Just as your partner's good stuff is also yours, so is the bad stuff. Taking responsibility for your partner's actions does not mean taking the blame but is instead an opportunity to recognize, accept, and work with those negative parts of yourself. In a marriage where this type of re-union with the separated halves is actualized, the couple will have a fertile and creative interplay that allows them to become whole people.

Creating a Handfasting Ritual

After you have understood the implications of uniting with your partner, the next step is to create a handfasting ritual that reflects and embodies the couple's dreams, ambitions, goals, and focus for their union. Most Pagans begin with a traditional handfasting ceremony, making alterations to personalize the rite.

First, you must decide whether you want a Year and a Day ceremony or whether you are involved in a relationship that warrants a more karmic bond. In addition, you must decide whether the handfasting will be a state-recognized marriage or whether an additional civil ceremony must be performed. The latter option is often chosen when relatives cannot accept alternative religions or when one of the couple is not Pagan. State laws also make a difference: in Colorado, "any minister"—a term loosely defined—can legally officiate at a wedding ceremony, but other states have stricter requirements, so a civil ceremony may be required in addition to a Pagan handfasting for the marriage to be legally binding.

I have included a sample handfasting ritual further on in this chapter; in addition, numerous others have been published. As with any magical operation, the elements of purification, circle-casting, statement of intention, and invocation will be present, but you may also wish to add a group attunement. Let us now look at these components in more detail as they apply to handfasting.

1. *Group Attunement:* In many cases not all wedding guests will be Pagans. In order to merge the diverse energies of all present into one that focuses and empowers the ritual, a group attunement is a good idea. Possible methods include a guided meditation, a moment of meditative silence, or a statement such as "As we prepare the sacred space for this marriage, let all of us take a few moments to meditate on the sacredness of love."

2. *Casting and Purification of the Circle:* Here you will want to use whatever methods you are already familiar with rather than creating something new and potentially confusing.

3. *Statement of Intention:* As in any ritual, you must briefly state your purpose. In addition, doing so will help non-Pagans present to understand what is taking place. For example, someone could say, "We are here today to celebrate, to witness, to bless, and to receive the blessing of Jim and Jane's handfasting."

4. *Invocations:* In a handfasting the invocations both invite the presence of the God and Goddess and receive their blessing on the marriage. In the case of an Eternal Ceremony, as opposed to the Year and a Day Ceremony, you may choose to draw into the handfasted couple the energies of the Divine Couple. This begins the *hieros gamos;* it is completed with the physical consummation later. The invocations may be the traditional Charge of the Goddess and the God, favorite poetry, or something written specifically for the marriage.

5. *The Commitment:* Here the bride and groom state before the Divine presence their commitment to the marriage and to one another in a manner similar to this:

> High Priestess: *Who comes to be joined in the presence of the Goddess? What is your name?*
> Groom: *My name is Jim.*
> High Priest: *Who comes to be joined in the presence of the God? What is your name?*
> Bride: *My name is Jane.*

6. *Symbolic Acts of Union:* Actions dating back to ancient times are still favored by modern Pagans. Here are some samples:

Handfasting: This is where the ceremony gets its name. The term derives from an old English custom of couples whose families disapproved of their marriage eloping to a town in Scotland for an informal but binding ceremony. The priest would join their hands and say something to the effect of "I now pronounce you man and wife." It was that simple.

In the Pagan version, the couple's hands are bound together with a knotted cord. The knot symbolizes union, eternity, and continuity. Using knots in marriage rites dates back to ancient Mesopotamia: priests in Sumeria took threads from the couple's garments and knotted them together as the climax of the ceremony.[5]

Crown of Flowers: Floral wreaths remind us of the crown of flowers worn by the woman in the Tarot card "Strength" and symbolize the magical circle, eternity, and fertility. The wreath is often charged with the four magical elements—fire, earth, air, and water—to bring balance to the union. It may be passed over the kneeling couple's heads in an infinity sign (like the numeral 8 turned sideways) to represent their connection to the Divine Marriage.

Rings: Another symbol of wholeness and eternity, the wedding ring traditionally is placed on the third finger of the left hand because the ancient Romans believed that a vein or nerve led directly from this finger to the heart. The ring is also related to an ancient Celtic custom of passing the hands through a holey stone to symbolize the sanctity of a pledge.[6] Metaphysically speaking, the left hand is the hand of the internal person and of potential; the third finger is the finger of Apollo, representing self-expression, relationships with others, and personal power.

Jumping the Broom: Another form of the magical wand, the broom represents new beginnings, purification, and transformation. Prior to our own handfasting, my wife and I were amused when a fundamentalist Christian family member asked us when we were going to "jump the broom." This Pagan custom has been retained as a colloquial rural expression. In the handfasting rite, the broom is placed in front of the couple, who then jump over it to begin their new life together. The priestess then sweeps behind them to purify and to break old ties.

Confirmation by Participants: At the close of the ceremony, one of the officiants summarizes the union that has occurred, and the participants confirm by saying, "So mote it be."

Consummation: Though not an actual part of every handfasting ceremony, the physical consummation can take place if the couple so desires. While guests begin feasting and merrymaking, the couple retires to a private place to make love, hoping that when they return there will still be some food left! This sacrament confirms the couple's recognition of their spiritual identity: their union with each other as well as with the Goddess and the God.

Mundane Planning for Your Handfasting

While the handfasting ceremony can be as simple or complex as the participants desire, physical details must be attended to early on.

Depending where you live, the time of year may dictate whether the site is indoors or outdoors, but many Pagans prefer handfastings to occur outdoors in the sanctuary of Mother Earth. Possible locations include friends' yards, local parks, or state and national forests. If you chose the back yard, consider the neighbors, if there are any. If they are not already familiar with your religious preferences, is this already emotionally charged day the time you would choose to introduce them to it?

A similar situation may arise when using a municipal or county park. These may offer both attractive settings and covered pavilions that can be rented for the day. Your handfasting ceremony is a legal and permitted use, but remember that you are initiating a spiritual union, not making a political statement.

National and state forests can provide the most privacy and latitude for ritual expression. Check with the appropriate U.S. Forest Service or state forestry department office about those campgrounds that are rented to groups by the day. Fees are usually reasonable. Consider driving time and how difficult it may be fore guests to find the site. One possible drawback is the weather: if it rains, do you have a contingency plan or friends who "work weather"?

If you prefer an indoor ritual, you have several options. Many Pagan handfastings have been held in Unitarian churches. You may also check the yellow pages under "Halls" for spaces to rent. Most churches or halls must be reserved at least two months in advance. Be sure that the room you use has a large open area for your circle without view-obstructing pillars. Check the sensitivity of the smoke alarm if you plan to use incense: we attended one handfasting at a Unitarian church where the smoking incense set off the alarm. Needless to say, the shrieking alarm and the firemen's arrival disrupted the ceremony.

The ritual's timing is also important. Check an ephemeris to avoid planning when Mercury is retrograde, which can lead to communication difficulties, outbreaks of Murphy's Law, transportation hassles, and other snags, or when Venus is retrograde, which can signify emotional excess, misunderstandings, and sudden unexpected tears. Periods when the Moon is "void of course" (in other words, making no major aspects before it leaves a sign) should also be avoided; projects started at these times tend to bog down. Positive astrological factors include trines and sextiles between the Moon and Venus, Neptune, Mercury, Sun, and Jupiter, and between Venus and Jupiter, Sun, Mercury, Mars, and Neptune.

Consider your guests. If some are not Pagan, someone may need to explain aspects of the ritual to them and what is expected of them. Non-Pagan guests are often concerned about "different" activities and behaviors. You may wish to write a brief explanation of the ritual and what guests should wear and bring to send out with invitations. Explaining things before the rite is another possibility, but can prove frustrating if people arrive at the last minute.

Other factors to take into account in planning include such as these: Will the bride and groom have attendants, and what duties will they perform? If the space is small and attendants are stationed at each quarter, will the guests be unable to see? Will guests be seated or standing? Outdoor rites are generally simpler if the guests stand; otherwise, someone must lug 50 chairs to the park.

Once the physical details of your handfasting are worked out, you are ready to embark on perhaps your greatest journey. The rite of handfasting is an initiation into supreme transformation through love and sacrifice. There is no other magick like that to be found in marriage, for it is a Divine Creation that allows us to see far beyond ourselves. A handfasting may be the most significant ritual that one can take part in, for it will affect every aspect of life. This transformative power should be remembered when considering marriage, for many mysteries will be presented to and played out in the partners' psyches. Some lessons will be painful, some joyful, some sorrowful, and some enlightening, but all will be powerful harbingers of wisdom.

Concerning Divorce

No discussion of marriage would be complete without addressing the subject of divorce. Any relationship experiences ebb and flow, fertile times and stagnant times, beginnings and endings. This is not to say that a marriage will inevitably end in divorce, but only that the one constant in life is change. Sometimes changes necessitate endings in order to make room for growth.

In the Year and a Day Ceremony, a graceful ending is built in, for at the end of that period the couple can elect freely to do one of three things: end the relationship and go separate ways, commit to another year and a day, or commit to an eternal joining.

When the couple has been eternally joined on the other hand, the assumption from the start is that the marriage is to be permanent, made not only for this lifetime but perhaps for lifetimes to come. Sometimes, however, in the heat and excitement of their initial courtship two people decide on such a momentous ritual, only to discover later that they had only limited lessons to learn together.

This realization can bring pain and disillusionment. But once they resolve that an ending is the most positive answer to their dilemma, the healthiest action is to to perform a Parting of the Ways ritual. The couple may write their own ritual or engage a third party to help them with it. The ceremony need not be long, but it should contain these elements:

1. *Statement of Intention:* The intention is to let go of the relationship and with grace and integrity to cut the bonds formed at the original marriage ceremony and during its duration.

2. *Symbolic dissolving or cutting of the bonds:* This may involve the same symbolism as the handfasting, but with the cord around the wrists now cut or the rings removed. Other ideas might be to blow out two candles that represent the couple or to have them face each

other while someone else cuts between them with the ritual knife from head to foot.

3. *Release of the energy:* In any ritual, energy raised must be released for the ritual to work. Holding onto any part of it allows tendrils of the bonds to regrow and entangle the parting couple.

A Parting of the Ways ritual does not erase any karma that remains to be balanced between the couple. It does not "clear the slate." What it does is free them to reintegrate themselves as individuals. If a civil marriage ceremony was also performed, a civil divorce decree must also be obtained. Likewise, if the couple has presented themselves as married in a state where common law marriage is recognized, they will need to be legally divorced.

Handfasting Rite

Attunement

  High Priestess (HPS): *As we prepare the sacred place for this marriage, let all of us take a few moments to meditate on the sacredness of love.*

Casting the Circle

The circle is cast and purified with the four elements. HPS and High Priest (HP) stand behind the altar. A door is cut in the northeast for the couple to enter. The Maiden leads attendants to their positions, then leads in the bride and groom. The circle is re-closed. Bride and groom stand before the altar facing east, bride on left and groom on right. They kneel.

Statement of Intent

  HPS or HP: *We are here today to celebrate, to witness, to bless, and to receive the blessing of* (name) *and* (name's) *handfasting. Together they weave their commitment with trust, support, and with fidelity. It is a commitment based in love, in affection, and in an instinctive bonding between two people. This bonding is of the physical body, is of the human personality, and is of the inner, spiritual being.*

(Turning toward the couple) *Marriage is the most intense of human relationships wherein the partners act as mirrors for one another. Where you sow or expect hurt, misunderstanding, rejection, or isolation, so you will find it in each other. But where you sow or expect love, trust, generosity, support, and affection, so you will find these qualities in one another. Know that when you love each other perfectly, you will have grown to loving all life perfectly.*[7]

Invocations

HP: *Let us now lift up our hearts and our consciousness as we call to the Great Mother of all things that through her we might find the highest ideals of love and of marriage—and let these ideals incarnate now in this time and place.*

She who has been called among humanity Isis, Artemis, Astarte, Aphrodite, Cerridwen, Arianrhod, and many other names: may we now receive her words.

HPS: *Come to me whenever you have need of anything, when your hearts might fill with shadow, for I am the Queen of all wisdom. And you shall be free in spirit, and as a sign that you are really free you shall dance, sing, feast, make music and love. all in my praise. For mine is the ecstasy of spirit, and mine also is joy on earth, for my law is love unto all beings. Keep pure your highest ideal; strive ever towards it. Let nothing stop you or turn you aside. For mine is the secret door which opens upon the Land of Youth, and mine is the cup of the wine of life and the Cauldron of Cerridwen, which is the Holy Grail of Immortality. I am the gracious Goddess, who gives the gift of joy unto the heart of humankind. Upon earth, I give the knowledge of the spirit eternal, and beyond death I give peace and freedom and reunion with those who have gone before. I am the mother of all living, and my love is poured out upon the earth.*

HP: Hear the words of the Star Goddess, she in the dust of whose feet are the hosts of heaven and whose body encircles the universe.

HPS: I who am the beauty of the green earth, and the white moon among the stars, and the mystery of the waters, and the desire of the heart, call unto your soul. Arise and come to me. For I am the soul of nature, who gives life to the universe. From me all things proceed, and unto me all things must return; and before my face, beloved of gods and of people, let your innermost divine self be enfolded in the rapture of the infinite. Let my worship be within the heart that rejoices; for behold, all acts of love and pleasure are my rituals. And therefore let there be beauty and strength, power and compassion, honor and humility, mirth and reverence within you. And you who think to seek for me, know your seeking and yearning shall avail you not unless you know the mystery: that if that which you seek you find not within yourself, you will never find it without. For I have been with you from the beginning, and I am that which is attained at the end of desire.

HP: *Great Pan, Lord of the Arcadian paradise! Inspire our hearts with your presence. Thrill our hearts with your pleasant notes. Answer our wills with your perfect magick. Let the woods and fields, mountains and valleys, find protection in your footsteps. Let hare and hawk, otter and badger, the vixen and her cubs, and all the families of our brothers and sisters of the wild find comfort in your touch. Let the birds of the air and the bats of the night dance freely to your piping, and the fish of the rivers and the great seas find peace at the echo of your call. Let all small things nestle secure against your mighty legs, protected by the goat-footed God.*[8]

Bright Sun, Dark Death, Lord of Winds, Lord of the Dance, Sun Child, Winter-born King, Hanged One, Untamed Lord, Stag and Stallion, Goat and Bull, Sailor of the Last Seas, Guardian of the Gate, Ever-Dying-Ever-Living, Radiance, Dionysus, Osiris, Cernunnos, Ra, Thoth, Arawn, Triple God of Youth, Seeker, and Wise Mage, bring your blessing to this marriage![9]

(The bride and groom stand and are doubly purified with oil and then with lips.)

HPS: *Who comes to be joined in the presence of the Goddess? What is your name?*
Groom: *My name is _____.*
HP: *Who comes to be joined in the presence of the God? What is your name?*
Bride: *My name is _____.*

HPS: (Name) *and* (name), *we greet you with joy.*

(Bridge and groom kneel again. HP joins the couple's hands while HPS fastens cord around their wrists.)

HP: *As your hands are joined with this cord, know it is your will to be united and to love and cherish one another through all lifetimes.*

(HPS takes crown of flowers from altar and charges it with the four elements. She passes it over the groom and bride's heads in the infinity sign, then places it on the bride's head.)

HP: *O ye Guardians of the Gate, O powerful God, O gentle Goddess, witness now the union of these two! By this Magick Circle, by Earth, Air, Fire, and Water, by the Sun, by the Moon, and their children the Stars do these souls come together to share life in its sorrow, its joy, sharing strength, peace, and wisdom! In perfect love and perfect trust, equal before one another.*
HPS: *I take you to my hand, my heart, and my spirit by the strength of the Sun and the magick of the Moon.*

(Groom repeats those words and places ring on bride's finger.)

HP: *I take you to my hand, my heart, and my spirit by the strength of the Sun and magick of the Moon.*

(Bride repeats those words and places ring on groom's finger.)

(The Maiden brings a broom and lays it in front of the couple. They both jump over it and kiss HP and HPS, then each other. HP traces pentagram in front of them, and HPS sweeps away all negativity behind them with the broom.)

(Bride and groom take up platter of cakes from the altar and together say:)

> *In recognition of our physical union, we bless these cakes.*

(Bride and groom take up wine and say:)

> *In recognition of our spiritual union, we bless this wine.*

(They offer it to HPS, who drinks, then likewise HP, Bride, Groom, and Maiden. Bride and groom then take cakes and wine to the north quarter and offer them to each of the celebrants. All return to altar.)

> HP: *Let the Sun and the Moon and the Stars and these our loved ones bear witness that* (name) *and* (name) *have been joined together in the sight of the God and Goddess. And may the God and Goddess bless them as we do ourselves.*
> ALL: *So mote it be!*

Music begins. Bride and groom are led away to consummate the handfasting (if desired) while the festivities begin.

ABOUT THE AUTHOR

Handfasted himself in 1991, Jeff Charboneau-Harrison is a painter, writer, and musician. He works to integrate magickal study and application into his artistic vision. In addition to his Pagan spirituality, he has a long-time interest in Qabalah and Hermetic teachings. He looks to weave together the beauty, celebration, and Victorious "force" of Pagan magick with the clarity, practicality, and splendid "form" of Qabalistic magick. In this vein he is working with his wife Karen on a book titled *Integrative Magick: A Practical Ceremonial Approach for the 21st Century.*

NOTES

[1]Joseph Campbell. *The Power of Myth*. (New York: Doubleday, 1988), 6.

[2]Thorwald Dethlefsen, quoted in Gerd Ziegler. *Tarot: Mirror of Your Relationships* (Neuhausen: Switzerland: Urania Verlags AG, 1989), 9

[3]Campbell, 6

[4]Edwin Steinbrecher. *The Inner Guide Meditation*. (York Beach, Maine: Samuel Weiser, 1989), 155.

[5]Ethel Urlin. *A Short History of Marriage*. (New York: Rider and Son, 1913), 95.

[6]Urlin, 156.

[7]William Bloom. *Sacred Times: A New Approach to Festivals*. (Findhorn: Findhorn Press, 1990), 37–8.

[8]Janet and Stewart Farrar. *The Witches' God*. (Custer, Washington: Phoenix Publishing, 1989), 79.

[9]Starhawk. *The Spiral Dance*. (San Francisco: Harper and Row, 1979), 93.

Photo © 1993 Malcolm Brenner / Eyes Open

Puberty Rites
for Adult Women

by Oz

A group of women sat in the ritual circle and began to talk about why they were really there. Within minutes every woman in the circle was in tears. A young woman told about the physical and sexual abuse that she had suffered as a young child and the threats that kept her silent. She talked about how that abuse affected the way that she felt about herself as a woman and how different she felt from everyone else in the circle. Another woman talked about her inability to respond sexually all her life and about her cold marriage. Another woman told how an uncle who used to babysit her had made her perform oral sex on him, telling her that this was the job of all women and that she never should talk about it. Others told of cruel mothers—one who even told her daughter repeatedly that she wished that she would die. Another's father had always called her "son" because he was so disappointed that she had not been born a boy. Another was ostracized by other girls in her neighborhood because of her parents' religion. One woman told of being raped by some of her male high school classmates. She had tried to tell the school authorities but was not believed, probably because the boys were outstanding athletes while she was a "nobody."

This was no special circle. It might have been any of many circles. The same thing happens these days in many places, at many times. The stories are common in almost all circles, all gatherings of women—Pagan and otherwise. The truths that are finally being told are often far worse than those described here, and most women can tell of at least some verbal or mental abuse suffered by simply being a woman in this society. I have seen and felt—as one of the few whose life was relatively spared—tears of thankfulness, twinges of shame that I was so unaware, and deep sympathy for so many of my sisters. As a Witch I have been especially amazed to learn how the sacredness of my sisters' bodies and lives has been so violated.

Few of us grew up unscathed. Like other adult women today, most female Witches were raised in non-Pagan environments. There we were told that our bodies were dirty and that to touch ourselves was evil or nasty. We were embarrassed by puberty's changes. Our sexual education came through hasty, whispered conversations. Many of us were teased, harassed, or even physically abused during puberty. What was intended by the gods to be our time of blossoming often became more associated with physical and mental pain than with anything else. We have carried this shame into our adult lives, often facing a woman's life phases with trepidation and anxiety. Our menses, first lovemaking, childbirth, menopause—times we now know to be sacred—were times many of us lived through in fear and discomfort.

When we grew up, becoming a sexual person was a confusing and mysterious journey. Clouded in misunderstanding and motivated mainly by peer pressure, most of us literally stumbled into our first real growing-up experiences. The greater society's attitude toward sex, like its attitude towards death, has been to keep it hidden, relegated to the same unmentionable realms that hold other things "occult"; i.e., hidden. As women, our lives are intertwined with physical and emotional changes relating to our sexuality, and the messages we received in the past have added to our subconscious burdens of feeling that feminine = dark = lesser = unclean = weaker. The whole notion that "darkness" equals "evil" is philosophically inconsistent with a Witch's belief in a balance between feminine and masculine, dark and light—like the Taoist Yin and Yang. But despite our current philosophy, we often carry within ourselves the scars of growing-up experiences that were completely contradictory to these beliefs. As Pagan and Wiccan adults, we now see that we must regenerate in ourselves not only healthy attitudes about sex and our bodies but also a healthy recognition of the spiritual role that this takes in a wholly balanced life. Certainly, Pagan women are not unique in seeing the need for change nor in talking about it nor even in doing something about it. For us, however, the transformation must take place upon several planes at once. We do not seek just to heal our minds and emotions by talking or therapy. We bring the need to heal into the sacred circle of our rites. This need becomes a part of the practice of our religion and one more relinking of our real lives with our actual spirituality.

The Pagans of the world—our European and Mediterranean ancestors as well as the indigenous people of every time and place—had a different approach to the changing aspects of physical life than the one we grew up with. Theirs was not separate from their world of spirit. Life transitions were marked by celebrations, initiations, education, and camaraderie. The time of puberty, the changes of menopause, and preparations for death were occasions when ages of accumulated wisdom and traditions were shared, enacted, and passed on to those who were approaching their own changes. Each person's metamorphosis, therefore, became a joining with those who had gone before rather than a time of isolation and fear. Becoming was also belonging. The sacredness of the totality of life was reaffirmed by the fact that religion, spirit, and God-beings were inseparable factors in every aspect of mortal reality, including all "mundane" or "earthly" machinations of the physical body.

Today we seek to reclaim this heritage of wisdom-ways. As Neopagans and modern Wiccans, we have learned to attune ourselves to the changes that are the cycles and seasons of all of nature. We celebrate the Wheel of the Year—summer to fall to winter to spring again. In so doing we learn of the spring times, summers, autumns, and winters of our own lives. We observe the ebb and flow of the lunar tides, rising to full and waning to new, and we feel their effects within us. We become aware that we, who are life forms, are just as much a part of this cyclical and spiraling movement as is any other part of creation. As we observe the seasons and tides of nature with our rites and celebrations, so have we come to observe the times of transition inside ourselves with similar honorings. The saying "As above, so below" has meaning here: as the earth changes, so do our bodies. As we celebrate the turnings of the planet, so do we celebrate the turnings of the self.

A natural outgrowth of this awareness has been an evolution of new rites, genuine Mysteries. We have sat much and contemplated the mysteries of life. We have found that this is the mystery: life itself—our real lives and the inherent mysteries of birth, growth, change, and death. The time we have spent considering and meditating upon the "greater" mysteries of the universe has brought us back to our own backyards. Our Goddess says, "For if that which you seek you find not within yourself, you will never find it without."

Now we begin to apply what we have learned to ourselves. Neopagan women have dared to peek behind the veil of obscurity into what has been lost to our people for many generations. Out of a gradual exploration of our spiritual femininity has come an inspiration like the words of the Seeress speaking for Gaia Herself. The ancient and new message is about our bodies, our lives, our girlhoods, our babies, our lovers, and the way that all our spiritual selves are involved with the realities of life. Once again, the women's rite becomes a powerful force for change.

When we first began putting together women's rites, we experimented with many symbols. We painted one another's faces and bodies, sang songs to the Goddess, hugged and chanted in our mutual agreement of the rightness of being female, and crawled through tunnels comprised of the legs of women standing closely front to back—the birth canal. Through exploring images of women and Goddess, digging into the dark recesses of our feminine subconscious (at first shallowly), we unearthed a great need for healing. Now it is time for our rites to come together in ways that go beyond the mere enactment of symbols into a deep exploration of our own psyches. We have at our disposal everything in our Witch's bag of tricks which we can pull out and aim at the really scary parts of ourselves: the pasts we have tried to hide or forget. We can borrow from the puberty rites of indigenous cultures and incorporate what we have learned in encounter groups, sensitivity training, Masters and Johnson workshops, Gestalt therapy, and Neuro-Linguistic Programing. We already have chants and songs, we know how to drum ourselves into trances, and we are able through visualization to regress ourselves into those pasts. We have worked with Jungian "active imagination" and know ways to reprogram the subconscious through symbol and ritual. To guide and assist us, we call upon the Goddess who is the Divine Feminine herself, protector and healer of all women. She is called in Her united form of All-Goddess or in one of Her many faces. Sometimes we may draw Her down with the Moon into the circle of all-women and let Her speak to us.

With this inspiration, we are beginning to recreate the rites for our own daughters and for the passages yet to come in our own lives. Puberty rites are again being celebrated for our young, and ceremonies created to honor menarche, sexual initiation, motherhood, menopause, and cronehood. Yet those of us who are adults now still yearn for a life that has been wholly made sacred and feel that a part of our soul-past is incomplete. For some, the answer comes in a vital neo-traditional ritual concept: the adult puberty rite. In this ceremony a woman is able to receive for herself recognition that she might have benefited from in her youth—had she received such an honoring at that time.

The experience psychologically and magickally "replaces" a coming-of-age that may have been less than desirable, thus helping to heal both the adult woman and her inner child self.

In such a ceremony, a woman might first be taken through a period of verbal or visualized exploration of her own youth, as much as is needed to get her in touch with and communicating about that time of her life. She is taken back into that time and brings a part or sense of her youthful consciousness back into the present. For some, childhood, puberty, or early womanhood may have held trauma. For others, the transition may not have been experienced or acknowledged in a positive way. Even a woman who did not necessarily have negative experiences may feel a desire to sacralize a time of her life that was so pivotal in developing her personality and attitude towards her own femaleness. Ritual can provide a safe space in which to reintegrate, recreate, or reconsecrate this past. In current abuse-survivor therapy, techniques employed often include an imagistic or magickal return to the times that need reliving. Past-life regression therapy uses similar techniques of reviewing and rescripting experiences from our pasts in order to heal the effects of difficult experiences. Witches often use similar ritual techniques for healing themselves and others, combining visualizations with symbolic drama and intentionally willed focus. Any similar method may be used as part of an adult woman's puberty rite.

The ritual goes a step further by next actually taking the woman through an initiation. She is given the puberty rite that she never had when she was young. A safe space is created by the encouragement and sympathy of women who share and understand. At this time very powerful energies of caring, love, and common support can be raised by the women in the circle into a a cone of healing power to be applied as a soothing potion to psychic wounds, scars, and self-doubts. Both the present woman-self and the past child-self are consecrated by a mystical force comprised of the woman's own newfound strength, the passionate compassion of her sisters, and the divine spiritual light of the Goddess. Undesired elements from a woman's past can symbolically be allowed to die or be transmuted while a new, whole, and sacred woman arises from the circle, the "cauldron of rebirth." Part of this resurrection is created simply by a validation of the woman's intrinsic internal knowing as she comes to see her own femaleness as beautiful, honorable, worthy, and empowered.

The greater part of the transformation, however, cannot be described in terms either literal or psychological. When the actual magick happens, as it frequently does, no words can convey either the reality or the direct cause of the experience. If the rite is effective, a moment of change comes—sometimes as an instant mystical flash, sometimes gradually, settling in as a new perspective in the woman's entire being. Just as with other miraculous phenomena, only those who have had such experiences themselves will be able to understand the reference. Those who come out reborn are changed forever.

In one such rite, the magick has begun even before the circle is entered. The room is dark except for a few candles, and bright lights of the city below glitter in the picture windows. On the floor, a circle is outlined with a border of lace; carpets and cushions are spread inside its perimeter. Statues of women and goddesses stand on the altar together with bouquets of flowers. There is a heavy scent of roses and an entrancing music of harps and drums. Many women are already in the circle, some holding hands, several giggling, and a few crying tears of happiness.

One woman, wearing a silver crown and a long, flowing, red robe, steps outside the circle and towards the closed double doors. There is a hush; movement within the circle stops. The priestess slowly opens the doors, and the scraping sound of wood seems louder than possible. A woman stands on the other side, draped in a white gown and colored scarves. She is blindfolded and trembling. A companion who has guided her to the door holds strongly to her arm.

"Are you ready to enter the circle of women?" the priestess asks. There is a long hesitation before the answer comes, and the woman in white reaches out hesitatingly with her hands, blindly seeking something to hold onto. She is guided gently to the circle's edge. She has been through a day of difficult emotion, memories, and tears in preparation for taking this step. She is still a bit shaky. Her blindfold is removed, and she sees a room full of beautiful images and the faces of many women who are all her friends, each one smiling. The priestess anoints her forehead and beckons her into the circle. She joins her sisters, who hug her in turn and begin to dance slowly to the rhythmic music. Her trembling is replaced by a new feeling of acceptance, confidence, and grace as she begins to dance with the others. Whatever may have happened in her life journey before this point, she has survived and now may claim her courage and her strength. Her rite of becoming a woman is beginning.

What may happen within such rituals is as varied as the women who perform them. Creativity, inspiration, and realization are sparked by the Muses, the magick, and the moment. Women who never thought of themselves as talented may discover an ability to paint, sing, draw, write poetry, or dance. Some find within themselves an urge to dress in flamboyant costume or to create artistically pleasing environments and tools for the ceremony. Out of the frustration of growing up in a world that has made it tough to be female, women often find that they have developed an untapped inner resourcefulness. In the new women's circles they can apply these abilities to a meaningful purpose. Here they create a place into which the Goddess is not only invoked but may feel truly honored by seeing Her own reflection in the childlike wonder of women discovering themselves. Here their imaginations may safely run wild without fear or shame.

Women want to reclaim the joy and rightness that should have been part of all their lives' phases. They say to one another, "Here, this is the way I wish it had been for me, and this is the way I want it to be now." For today's Pagan and Wiccan women these statements become just as much declarations of their spiritual paths as expressions of their emotional healing and of their politics. Making these statements is in itself a coming-of-age for us. We have already learned that our time together as women can and must be more than a time to gossip or denigrate others (male or otherwise). Now we begin to know just how much power we have available to us, how much force our innately intuitive beings carry. We are the power to transform and to rebirth, for this is our birthright. Women are change: we live change, our bodies change, and we can make change. We are like Changing Woman, a goddess of the Navajo people, whose very strength is that She is never the same. She is the personification of the shifting sands that comprise the face of the Mother Earth, and She teaches us to use the shifting physical and emotional realities that we as women carry throughout our lives. We learn from Her and from all goddesses that we are like the Moon, that we are like the seas, and that we need not ever be a way that we do not wish to be once we realize and actualize our natural potentials.

We only need to remember that we do have the power to change both ourselves and the world we live in and that in our rites and ceremonies we can begin to make it right. With rites such as these we can even change our pasts and in so doing perhaps help to change the future for all women.

ABOUT THE AUTHOR

Oz has been practicing and teaching ritual and the Ways of the Goddess for 23 years. Her background includes Western esotericism, Wicca, Yoga, Middle Eastern dance, music, and many new forms of magick. She has led rites of all types and sizes at different locations in the United States, including blessing newborns, personal transitions, and group celebrations. As a priestess dedicated to Hekate, Inanna, and Isis, she leads workshops and rituals to help people connect more vividly with the Goddess in these aspects.

Reweaving the Web

Pagan Approaches
to Illness, Grief, and Loss

by Paul Suliin

On December 31, 1984, I was attending a New Year's Eve party at a hotel in Chicago. I had brought along my Tarot deck, and I was giving readings to those guests who expressed an interest. A woman named Fran asked me to lay out the cards for her, and we found a quiet corner.

I make it a practice not to ask my querents what their questions are until after the cards are laid out. This spread was among the most unforgiving that I have seen. I looked over the cards, and a dim intuition began to form.

I asked Fran for her question. She looked worried for a moment. It seemed that her mother had just recently been hospitalized, and Fran was asking about her mother's health. My intuition clicked into full form, and I had to make a decision. After a long moment of soul-searching, I said, "Fran, I'm sorry, but my feeling is that your mother is going to die, probably within six weeks."

Fran and I spent the next couple hours just talking. It was snowing heavily, and a lot of the partygoers chose to take rooms in the hotel to weather the storm. Fran and I took a room together, and I spent the night holding her and talking some more.

Over the next several weeks, Fran and I spoke often by phone and in person, trying to help her deal with her mother's failing health. Fran's mother died in early February, just over five weeks after that New Year's Eve. Fran told me then and later that while it could never be easy, the several weeks she had been given to prepare and our many talks had helped her handle her grief more easily. This was my first experience as an adult with the reality and impact of grief and the loss of a loved one. It also showed me the power and relevance of the Pagan way in dealing with these issues.

As I write this it is hard to know who may eventually read it. The largest group will surely be those for whom this chapter is just one part of a larger work. I hope that to you I may offer some small understanding of grief and the ways in which it may someday touch your life. I can tell you that loss touches everyone sooner or later, and I know that recognizing and preparing for it can go a long way toward reducing its impact.

The Pagan religions emphasize health and wholeness for their members. Herbal medicine and magical healing are important parts of what we do, but it's equally important to learn the healing of less-tangible hurts. I hope that some of what I say here will help you when you one day face a loss in your own life.

If you are trying to support a friend or a loved one through a difficult time, then I hope that I can help you understand what they are feeling. I must tell you now that you cannot heal their pain, however good your intentions; only they can heal themselves, and that only with time. However, there are things that you can do to help them at it, and there I may be able to offer some suggestions.

If you have suffered a recent loss yourself, then let me say that I am sorry. I won't say "I understand how you feel" because no one really can, and you're probably tired of hearing that. But although this is perhaps cold comfort now, I can say that the pain will ease. And it may be that understanding what you are feeling and why will make it at least a little easier. So please, do read on.

The Buddha said that the world is sorrow. We might not go quite that far, but we can agree that grief is one of the few truly universal human experiences. Sooner or later, everyone is touched by loss. Yet few care to face it. It's more comfortable to pretend that pain is "out there" somewhere, happening to other people, and will never invade our lives. In part, this is because just trying to imagine how we might cope with a serious loss or illness can bring on many of the same feelings of fear and despair that the loss itself can cause. But as a result most of us are ill-prepared to deal with tragedy when it does come calling. The pain of loss is bad enough under any circumstances. Coming to it with no preparation makes it that much worse, and the healing process takes that much longer.

All right then, what is grief? It is a response to bereavement, the "cutting away" of a part of our lives and ourselves. Each one of us is at the center of a complex web of interrelations and interactions which define and shape our lives. The loss of a loved one, a job, a home, or any of the the most important parts of our lives cuts us off from a portion of that web, like a spiritual amputation. We suddenly find ourselves missing a part of the network that makes us what we are. Relationships and feedback which had helped define our lives are suddenly gone. The pain and confusion, the sense of loss and the blind, groping feeling that result are what we experience as grief.

Grief is seldom found alone, especially in major losses. It's often alloyed with fear, for if our lives could be so drastically altered, what might not happen next? A sense of hopelessness or despair is also common, as we face going forward without a spouse, a parent, or trusted friend. There is anger and guilt, and even relief, depending on the nature of the relationship and the circumstances of the loss. All of these feelings and more may be wrapped together around the loss, and each must be unpacked and dealt with before the wound can heal.

And healing is absolutely necessary. If this wound does not heal well, or if it never really heals at all, it can affect the victim for many years to come. Like a physical wound, a grief wound must either heal, or fester. Repressed or unhealed grief acts like an emotional blockage. It can result in lowered creativity, a feeling of deadness, depression, even physical (psychosomatic) illness. As the healing is delayed, the victim may become almost accustomed to these problems. Unhealed grief comes to feel almost "normal," as the psyche wraps itself around the wound like a tree growing over a spike.

Always remember that bereavement is not only caused by death. Any serious disruption in our lives can damage the web and set us adrift. Some of the most common causes of grief are:

• Death of a relative or loved one—This is surely one of the most common and best-known bereavements. Those we love and those who love us form a major part of the web that defines our lives. We see ourselves in their eyes and through our relationships with them: We are husbands to our wives, daughters to our mothers, fathers to our sons, and confidantes to our friends and counselors.

• Lost Relationship—When a marriage or other loving relationship ends, it is a tragedy for all concerned. Many of us have have planned our lives around the future we hoped to build in that relationship. If we lose the relationship we lose that future, and we lose the person that we once loved enough to build our lives around. Not only that, but such a loss often arises from its own tangle of love, anger and other warring emotions that flow into and around the grief wound.

• Moving or loss of a home—This one often surprises people, but it shouldn't. "Home is Where the Heart Is" has its converse, that our hearts and our memories are in our homes. Our homes are the centers of our lives, the context in which everything else takes place. We think of ourselves as living in a certain place. If we lose that home through disaster or financial trouble we are faced with the fear and uncertainty of finding a new nest. Even if we move of our own accord we still have to reestablish the bond that comes with The Place Where We Live. Until we do we may often have to deal with a restless, lost feeling, a sense of being set adrift.

• Loss of a job—When you think of what you are, what role you fill in life, many times one of the first roles that comes to mind is the one you fill at work.. When someone asks me "What do you do?" I may well answer "I'm a chemist," or "I'm a writer." And of course, many of us are the wage-earners, the financial support for our families. The loss of our livelihood, through layoff or prolonged illness, for example, breaks those strands of the web that define those roles in our lives. Not only that, but we must also deal with the worry and uncertainty of living without income, for however long it takes us to find new work.

• Serious illness—It seems that we can always say, "Well, at least I've got my health." But what if you don't? A sudden and/or prolonged illness, such as a stroke, a serious accident, or being suddenly disabled, is one of the most fundamental assaults on our self image. You probably don't think of yourself as someone who can see, or as someone who can fix your own dinner or cast a circle on your own—These are roles that all of us take, but we tend to take them for granted. But imagine, if you can, having that part of yourself abruptly taken away.

Of course, many other circumstances can cause this type of disruption. The basic principle in all cases is the damage to the web of our lives. Anything that breaks the relationships that define that web, or that requires new strands to be woven, can leave a grief wound. Even getting married or having a child can bring stress along with their joy—the web must be rewoven in all these cases, and many of the same emotions and principles apply in each.

With that need in mind, let's examine some of the more common feelings associated with grief and ways for dealing with them.

SORROW—This is the most obvious reaction, and one of the first to set in in many cases. A part of your life, of your self, is gone. Sadness is a perfectly normal, healthy reaction to this sort of trauma, but too often we try to "tough it out." We tell ourselves that someone else needs us to "be strong for them," or that our departed loved one would not want us to be sad. Well, it's entirely appropriate to feel sorrow when unpleasant things happen. Denying those feelings is like swimming against the tide: it tires you out fast and you seldom get anywhere. The Craft teaches us to live and work within nature, not against it, and this includes our own human nature as well.

In dealing with sorrow remember that it is normal. It is too easy to let yourself slip into despair (about which more later), a feeling that this overwhelming sadness will never end. It will, with time. The key to moving through sorrow is to let it run its normal course, to accept it and embrace it as your recognition that an important part of your life, your self, has gone. It is now up to you to make a new life in a new way. This is difficult, but not by any means impossible.

FEAR—If a sudden loss can take away your home, your job, or your loved ones, things that form the very base of your life and who you are, then what might not be next? Often, in the aftermath of bereavement, we may not think past our sorrow to face the other emotions that are wrapped up in it. We may fear for the future, but not even know that we fear, or what. But like sorrow, fear is a perfectly normal reaction to loss. It is not "unmanly," for example, or childish to admit to fear. In nature, fear serves a purpose: it is a reaction to danger or threat which helps make us ready to fight or flee.

In dealing with fear, look at it closely: is there anything real here to worry about—some financial problem that you need to address in the wake of a spouse's death, for example? If so, then make the solving of that problem a part of your recovery process. Once solved, it cannot frighten you any longer. But if a fear is more like "monsters under the bed," then take heart—there is nothing there to be afraid of. You might want to look at these unreasoning fears a little more closely: what is it that gives them so much power over you? For example, if you find yourself frightened after the death of a spouse, and there is no good financial or other reason to be afraid, then ask yourself what you are afraid of. Are you really afraid of being alone? If so, why? Is it because you don't think you can support yourself, or because you're afraid you can't handle things by yourself? If you can track a fear like that down to its roots and show yourself that these underlying fears are just wrong, then you may be able to break free and actually come out better than when you went in.

The greatest danger in fear is not facing it and admitting it, but letting it fester. Fear that is not recognized can become paralyzing, because a fear that is recognized can often be seen as groundless, while an unmet fear will dog your steps and drag you back from the process of resuming your life after a loss.

DESPAIR—If the props have been kicked from beneath your life, it's hard to know how to go on. Things can often seem hopeless and without purpose. This is one of the cruelest of all emotions, and one of the hardest to win past: by its very nature it denies the hope of a better future or the chance that we will ever be whole again. But, by that same token despair is one of the emotions that must be challenged, not merely accepted. It is a destructive denial of life, and we cannot face it with less than the most fervent affirmations of life and hope.

ANGER—A part of the denial process. We become angry at everyone—ourselves, our family, the doctors or ministers who tried to help, the Gods, even the loved one who has left us. We may lash out, almost at random. This is another phase of the grief process. Knowing that it is coming can help to defuse anger, because when we see it coming and know it for what it is we can often blunt the edge of the rage. "Oh, yes," you might say, "this was due about now." That way you can let the anger pass without blowing up and hurting someone who does not deserve it.

GUILT—Guilt is anger directed inward. A question that often torments the bereaved is "Was I responsible?" If we were somehow involved in the loss, or think that we were, it's hard to avoid wondering if we might not have done something more or something different.

Guilt can be a terrible, deadening burden. It is often a phase of denial: guilt represents an attempt to find a meaning in a great loss, a purpose or cause of tragedy, even if it means laying the blame on our own shoulders. It does not belong there, you know. Trying to find "meaning" in what may have been a senseless tragedy is not helpful. Better to create meaning in our lives today by using the process of grief work to make ourselves stronger and healthier. In that way the tragedy itself becomes the seed of new growth, and that can become its meaning for us.

For example, it happens all too often that we don't know how important someone is to us until they're gone. At that point we may look back on our life and it's very tempting to fall into the trap of guilt, thinking "I never told her how much I loved her. I should have done more." Well, that may well be true, but what are you going to do about it? You can't change the past, but you can shape the future. Instead of beating yourself for some real or imagined failing, take this to heart as a lesson. Learn to remember that relationship for what it taught you—the value of a friend and the importance of expressing that friendship. Turning a guilt-trip around and asking "So what do I do about it?" is a good way to turn tragedy into promise for the future.

Another way to gain from a loss is to learn more about yourself. Chances are that as you move through the healing process you'll find that you are stronger than you ever thought you were. A loss that you thought you would surely never recover from can leave you more confident and better able to cope with other losses just by virtue of the fact that it does not destroy you. You'll also learn a lot about the web that shapes your life, and with that knowledge you can better decide what parts to keep and what parts might be shaping you in ways you don't like. Just knowing that the web is there can give you a new perspective on your life and what it means to yourself and others—you affect them through the web just as they affect you.

As I set to work on this article, I received an object lesson in my subject. A woman friend for whom I care very much (I'll call her Anne) told me suddenly that she wanted nothing more to do with me. She offered no explanation, simply cut off our relationship completely and refused to answer my calls. Anne was not dead, but in many ways she might as well have been, and I had to set about putting myself and my life back together. A lot of what I was feeling is common to grief reactions. Psychologist Bob Deits (see "Recommended Reading" at end of this chapter) identifies four stages to the grief reaction. In many ways they are analogous to the Wheel of the Year and the stages in the cycle of life:

- Shock and Numbness
- Denial and Withdrawal

- Acknowledgement and Pain
- Adapting and Renewal

These stages will come along a course of months or even years. Sometimes it may seem that you are rushing from one into another willy-nilly, while at others it may be all you can do to drag yourself through. Sometimes you may not even realize that you've made the shift from one to the next until the difference in your outlook comes upon you all at once. Yet despite this uneven, sometimes unpredictable progression, knowing what to expect is the first important step in dealing with it well when it comes.

- Shock and Numbness (Winter)—The first stage of the grief process is the winter of the soul. When loss first hits, the natural reaction is to shut down, to mask the first raw edge of pain by refusing to feel it. People who don't know what to expect may often wonder why they do not seem to be feeling anything. "Don't I care?" they may ask themselves. This is not insensitivity but a reaction to trauma, a part of the mind's natural defenses against pain. This initial numbness may last hours or days. Just know to expect it, and that it will pass.

Like the physical winter, this is a time to prepare, not a time to act. The shock of sudden loss is unlikely to leave you in any fit state for making important decisions, but nevertheless people often try. They feel like they ought to be "doing something," just to be "doing something," so often they make bad decisions or do things they later regret. Remember, winter is a time to draw back, to assess the coming year, and to prepare for spring. In this case, spring means the flowering of pain when the first thaw hits and we begin to truly come to terms with what has happened.

For me in my relationship with Anne, this stage lasted just a few hours. The shock hit like a bucket of ice water: Why was she leaving? What had I done? The numbness followed hard on its heels, and in my case it manifested as a cold determination to find out what was going on here. I was not dealing with the loss at all, but rather trying to fill in the emotional void with activity: phone calls to friends, trying to find out why she had cut off contact with me.

• Denial and Withdrawal (Spring)—Closely related to numbness is denial. This is a reaction of fear and anger. It is a refusal to come to grips with the facts of loss, because we fear that what has happened could destroy us. Denial is exactly what it sounds like: "This can't be happening!" But because at some level we know very well that it is happening, anger and withdrawal are also natural reactions.

In this stage, there is a tendency to pull back from life and from the world around us. Like an animal pulling into its den to lick a wound, in withdrawal and denial we shut ourselves away from the pain we are experiencing. Fatigue and depression are often the hallmarks of this phase of the grief process, the body and mind attempting to shut down in the face of fear and pain almost too great to stand. You may see your appetite go, or lose interest in friends, family, and work. Nothing seems important any more, and that old enemy despair is waiting to close over you like quicksand.

At this stage denial can take many forms. This is the time when physical ailments are most likely to strike: the psychosomatic outgrowths of pain and a lowered resistance to illness that often accompanies depression. You might find yourself raging at everyone and no one, especially yourself. There might be fruitless fantasies about "turning back the clock" to undo what has happened. You might have to remind yourself that when you wake up your loved one will not be beside you in the bed, or catch yourself waiting for them to return. And each time your denial is shattered by reality it makes it that much more tempting to just go away and refuse to cope.

If people get stuck in any phase of the grief process it is likely to be this one, the muds of spring. It is the hardest to move through on your own, but it is also the time when it's hardest to ask for help, because by its very nature it is a time when you are trying to avoid dealing with the problem. Now is when knowing what to expect in this process can literally save your life. Just knowing that this phase is coming can make it easier to deal with. When that stifling paralysis hits you can recognize it for what it is and know that if you keep moving through you will come out the other side. That, and knowing how important it is to reach out for help at this stage, even though it's the last thing you want to do, can make all the difference in the world for getting through. In fact, knowing what to expect as the winter's numbness begins to thaw, you might want to have a friend near at hand when the pain really hits and pulling back and shutting down begins to look more and more attractive.

In my own example, I found that denial came very close on the heels of shock. It took a long time for me to accept that Anne really was gone from my life, that this was not a joke. I even considered for a time that I might be having a bad dream and that I just had to wake up. No such luck, unfortunately. Luckily, I did reach out to others. I discussed the way I was feeling with several friends, originally by asking them if they could figure out why Anne did what she did. Nobody could offer much insight into that, but in the course of talking it over I began to come to terms with the feelings I originally tried to bottle up, and I learned that they were not such frightening things after all. Painful, yes, and hard to face, but talking past the rough spots made my life much easier.

You might be wondering why I am associating such a cold and dismal time with spring. First, it is because spring always starts off cold and dismal. But second, it is because the point of the grief process is renewal, like the new life that arises from Winter. And the first real step of that renewal takes us past and through the treacherous time of withdrawal. The pain of this phase is like the first pains of labor that will eventually lead to your rebirth.

• Acknowledgement and Pain (Summer)—As spring shades into summer there comes a period of storms and rain that lay the foundation for the true growth of the Summer months. Grief works in much the same way. You will know that you've entered the third stage of the process when you begin to fully feel and acknowledge the pain of the loss. One of the surest signs of this is the ability to cry. It may seem strange to those who have never suffered a great loss that it is really very hard to cry in the denial phase. Indeed, it's hard to feel anything at all, but the pain keeps intruding. That is what makes withdrawal such a hard cycle to break but, paradoxically, that same pain is what will eventually bring us out of denial and into acknowledgement.

Beginning to accept the pain of loss, to feel it fully and without reservation, is at once the hardest and the most vital step in recovery. When it hits full on for the first time, and you really face the reality that you cannot go back to the way things were, you may feel like you have suddenly taken a turn for the worse. The temptation to duck back into the "safety" of withdrawal can be overwhelming. Don't do it! That first shock of pain means you are getting better, not worse.

Now is the time to really begin talking through your feelings. A good friend, clergyperson, or a support group can do the most good at this point. Keep a close eye on your feelings now, and try to accept them as the natural outgrowths of the loss you've experienced. Try to find some time every day to take your soul out and look at it, give it a good brushing, then put it back with care.

You may find yourself asking "Why?" an awful lot now. Why did it happen? Why am I still alive? Why doesn't anyone understand what I am going through? This is fine. Asking why, even if you never get an answer that satisfies you, is a lot better than pretending these questions don't exist.

Remember also that this is not a neat process. Withdrawal and denial are easy and attractive options, especially at the beginning, and you will find yourself slipping back into those old patterns ever so often. In fact, in the beginnings of the third stage you may find yourself "testing the waters" in your mind—allowing the first hints of pain to slip through, then slamming the doors of denial once again, only to open them just a crack and peek out a bit later. Gradually, like the fitful change from spring to summer, you will find it easier to cope with your feelings and you will be less and less likely to try to duck for cover.

I felt that gentle shift myself in dealing with Anne's loss. As I learned to talk about it I learned that the pain was sharp but not unbearable. I learned a lot about myself and about how I react to loss, and I began to notice the warning signs of denial and to short-circuit those dangerous habits. Very slowly I began to accept that she was not coming back, that I would not talk or share with her again, and to accept what that meant for me and how much I would miss her.

•Adapting and Renewal (Autumn)—This is the harvest time. You will know that you have entered the final stage, the "home stretch" in grief recovery, when you begin to focus less on the pain of the moment and more on what lies ahead. You have acknowledged that the web of your life is damaged and begun to explore the nature and extent of that damage, and you are now looking for ways to rebuild.

Everything else in the grief process has been building to this stage. Now you can do the real healing work, the business of setting your life in order. In part, you will realize that you have survived one of the most terrible and trying times in your life. The simple fact of that survival can give you a new sense of calm and confidence. You have begun to achieve "grief fitness," an ability akin to physical fitness in that your spirit is stronger now and more sure that the pain of life will not destroy, but only temper it. You can feel more secure in making plans, and in fact it will be good for you to start looking ahead for ways to apply what you have learned. Try to make new friends, learn new skills, or take a trip—get back into the world and take up the reins of your life once again.

I noticed in my own case that I was beginning to try to understand what might have caused my breakup with Anne and to plan how I might avoid those mistakes in the future. "The future" was becoming a real idea for me again, and I knew I was getting better.

The analogy to the Wheel of the Year begins to wear a bit thin now, because there is not another long cold winter ahead. There will be times when you have to take special care, because grief recovery is a lifelong process and you can expect to feel new pangs every so often, more seldom as time goes on. But you have the measure of pain now; you know that it cannot harm you if you ride it through.

Getting Past Grief

There is only one way to get through grief, and that is to move forward. Easy for me to say, right? Nevertheless, the process of healing the wounds of bereavement is called "grief work" for a very good reason: It *is* work. It is an active process of taking charge in your life, not a passive process of accepting. Surviving a major loss and turning it into a means for growth and renewal means first choosing to live. It is as simple, and as hard, as that. You have to make the deliberate decision to move forward, to take control of the grief process rather than letting grief ride you into the ground. In a sense, the pain lets you know you're alive—if you stop moving, you die.

Do not be afraid to experience grief! The fear that grief will destroy you, that some things are just too much to bear, can keep you from moving into healing forever. It is not too much: you are a lot stronger than you think you are. Let each phase of the grief process unfold naturally, neither hurrying nor holding back, and be prepared to feel the powerful and often painful emotions that come with those stages.

Remember also that you do not have to face it alone. Be willing to reach out to others and talk about what you are feeling. Join a support group with others who are facing loss. If there isn't one in your area, consider starting one yourself. (Priests and priestesses, this is a good place for you to get involved.) Do not neglect your friends and family for support through hard times. It is a true thing that shared sorrow is lessened and shared joy increased. Never be afraid to ask for help; in fact, if this is hard for you make a special point of doing it.

Keep a journal. You know the stages of grief now, and it can be a help to mark your progress through the process of rebuilding the web. A journal also helps you to take your feelings out and look at them, deciding which ones will help you and which will hold you back. The journal is also the place to record the results of any ritual work you undertake to help you with the healing process.

You do not need to share your journal with anyone, so be as frank and as open as you can. Show yourself what is going on in your head and your heart. If you decide it would help, of course, you can always share part or all of your journal with a friend or with your priest/ess. This is always an option, but never an obligation.

Be kind to yourself. Remember that grief has a physical component as well, and physical effects. You may need more rest than usual, and you will need to take special care to eat properly. Exercise can also help. But remember balance as a Pagan virtue: don't overdo, or use grief as an excuse to cultivate unhealthy or obsessive habits. It's easy to slip into a pattern of using sleep, food, or drugs as an escape from dealing with our problems. Keep a sharp eye out for those habits and nip them in the bud.

Be kind to others. It's easy to forget that not everyone is feeling what you are, and friends and family may not know how to help. Even more, you may find that some people cannot deal with your grief! This is true, believe me. There will be people who don't want to talk about your loss, who will tell you that "it's not healthy to dwell on these things," or who will try to avoid talking to you at all. To them, you represent something that they would rather not face in their own lives. This is not your fault. A lot of it isn't even theirs, really. But be ready for reactions like these and for all kinds of other well-meant but insensitive behaviors. Don't push, or try to change them, but don't buy into any hurtful ideas that can stunt your healing, either. Be secure in yourself, and know what you need to do to get better.

Do not forget the other side of that coin, either. Other people in your life may be feeling the loss as well. This is not true only of those who might have been connected to the loss, such as other relatives who share your pain after a death in the family. Often, people you never expected may take your grief as hard as you do. Friends hurt for you, and they may not have the tools for dealing with these feelings effectively. Don't be afraid to offer to help. You may find that helping them rebuild is therapeutic for you as well.

Time, Time, Time

This is a vital ingredient in all grief work: it takes time. My loss of Anne's friendship took many weeks to move through, and recovering from a really major loss can take a long time indeed—three to four years is not unusual. But keep telling yourself that recovery will come. Also, bear in mind that progress is not necessarily steady. It is not at all unusual to be doing quite well, to feel that you are out the woods at last, only to hit the first anniversary of the loss, or to be reminded by a song, or a picture, or even a scent, and discover a whole new wellspring of emotion bubbling to the surface. This just means that there are things you haven't dealt with yet, or stages in the healing process that you haven't yet reached. Be ready for these when they come and they won't hit you nearly as hard.

Clergy in Grief Work

If a member of your circle is working through these problems you may feel that there is something you should be doing but you may not know what. Your role as a Priest or Priestess is limited largely by what your friend will let you do, but there are ways you can help if it seems appropriate.

First, just be available to talk. This is good advice for any friend of the bereaved, but a priest or priestess can be especially valuable in this regard, since the role you fill makes you a special counselor and confidant. And don't be afraid to say "I don't know"—the problems and questions that arise in grief work may tax the wisdom of Solomon, but admitting that you don't have the answers either is always better than offering phony advice that doesn't stand the test of time. Just being there to listen can often do more good than anything you might have to say in any case.

If it seems appropriate, you can work a healing rite for the bereavement into an esbat or sabbat. Religion can offer an anchor when we badly need one, and a rite in circle can be very healing for some people. Ask your circle member if this might help. If it seems so, then give it a try, but don't take it amiss if your friend doesn't want to go this route. Grief work is intensely personal, and what sounds good to you may not help as much as you think.

Pagan Suicide Counseling

One common response to grief is suicide or thoughts of suicide. If the situation following the loss of home or job seems hopeless, or life seems no longer worth the living without a loved one or dear friend, or if a serious illness is sapping one's strength and vitality, then thoughts of suicide are not at all unexpected. This in fact is one of the most dangerous effects of the more destructive grief-reactions, such as guilt and despair. Suicide should be addressed very carefully by anyone considering it, and by anyone trying to help a potential suicide.

If you are considering suicide, the very first advice I would offer is "procrastinate!" The decision to take one's own life is, I believe, the right of every lucid adult. However, it is arguably the most serious decision that we can ever make. Once it's carried out, it can never be corrected or unmade. So I urge anyone who is considering this to consider very carefully. You can always kill yourself tomorrow, if after thinking it through you decide that it is truly the best course for all concerned.

Are you taking this step with a clear mind? If you have just suffered a great shock or loss, are you sure that you are thinking everything through as carefully as this decision deserves? Always ask yourself—Is there no better purpose that your life could serve? Is there not some service that you can render to the Gods and to the world around you? And before you say "no," think again about the Gods' abilities to turn your life to Their purposes, if you place yourself in Their hands. If you are a priest or priestess then be especially careful, since your life is no longer all your own. When you assume the mantle of the clergy, you give over a part of yourself to the needs of the Gods and of your religious community.

Guilt is also a motive for suicide, but to my mind it is never a very good one. Will killing yourself undo anything that has happened? Probably not. Will it make you feel better? That looks like a silly question when it's put that way, and in fact it is, but many people approach suicide as that sort of solution before they think about it. If there is one thing that you simply must do when contemplating suicide, it is think about it very carefully.

The Will of the Gods

One of the most common, and in my opinion one of the most destructive, responses to grief is "It's part of the Gods' plan." I don't buy it. Yes, death is a natural part of life. Yes, the Gods have given us ways to turn death into new life through the cycles of nature and the turning of the year. But that does not mean that the pain and anguish of loss are of Their choosing. It does not mean that the Gods have taken our loved one away as part of some greater "plan" to "help us grow" or whatever the homily *du jour* happens to be. The love and support that come from the Lord and the Lady can indeed help us turn tragedy into triumph, but I ask you never to think that They wanted it this way.

The "problem of pain," or why the Gods allow such things to happen, is one that all religions have to face at some point. My wife Michele has given me the following myth to meet this problem:

The Lady created the universe because creation brings Her joy, and the lives and loves of Her creations are for Her an endless source of pleasure. But when the time for creation came, the Lady learned that nature was not all Hers to command: Certain conditions are imposed on any material world. The old must always give way to the new, if the new is to have room to grow to its full potential. Thus, death is a necessary part of life, to "clear the stage" for new growth. Likewise, some animals must kill and eat others to survive. A living planet will sometimes shudder in its development, and earthquakes, fire, and flood are sometimes the unavoidable consequences of the growth of mountains, the lightning of the storm, and the rain that waters a field. The laws of nature are such that not even a Goddess can countermand them.

But the Lady knew that amidst all the suffering there would be joy and life as well. So She chose to Create, knowing full well as She did so that She would feel with us all of our pain, cry with all of our tears, but also laugh with all of our joy. And She knew that She could teach some of us to hear Her laughter and to feel Her crying with us.

Now it falls to each of us as Pagans to make of this world the very best world it can be. We cannot avoid loss, but we can turn it around. We cannot dodge death, but we can let it help us rather than let it tear us down. And know always that the Gods are with you, lifting you up and helping you come out the other side stronger than before.

A Solo Ritual for Healing a Loss

Remember that healing takes time, and no amount of magick can change that. However, this ritual can help bring the healing process into sharper focus for you, and speed things along by recruiting your whole self into the effort.

Find a quiet time when you can be alone. The beginning of the waxing Moon is a good time for this ritual, but any time will do. Try to set aside a half hour or so, or more if you can.

If you can, find something that will remind you of the relationship lost in the bereavement. Get some paper, or possibly your ritual journal, and a pen or pencil.

Cast a circle in your preferred way. Once the space is consecrated, sit down and place your memento where you can see it (you can place it on your altar if you have one).

Now let your mind wander over the memories of the relationship. Let the images come and go as they will, but try to notice them and what they are telling you. Notice how you feel, and let those feelings come fully and honestly. Try to learn from these images and feelings the role that this relationship played in your life. How did it fit into the web of relations that defined you as a person? For example, if you have lost a loved one, were you friend, lover, husband, wife, father or mother to them? How did a lost job or an old home fit into the whole that made you what you were? Understanding what you've lost is a first vital step toward reweaving the web.

Write down what you're feeling if you can. You might try writing a letter to the person or thing you've lost. Express exactly how you feel—if you are angry, frightened, sad or lonely, write it down. No one ever need see this but you, but it will help more than you may know to get your feelings down on paper where you can see them.

Now think about what you might do to help your-self heal. It can be as fantastic or as practical as you like. If you have broken up with a lover, what might you do to get yourself back on track? Bearing in mind what you have lost, how might you replace that part of the web of your life? You can write this down too, possibly in the same letter, or separately as you wish, and once again remember that you are the only person who ever needs to see this; the point is once again to explore your feelings, and this time to explore some of your options as well. Some may be workable, others may not, but the important thing is to realize that you do have options.

When working in this ritual try to be mindful always of the love of the Lord and Lady. As the Charge of the Goddess says, "I am the Mother of all things, and my love is poured out upon the earth." The Gods are with you always, ready to bear you up and ease your pain if you'll only let Them. Remember that She hurts with you, and Their strength can bear you up when yours is almost gone.

When you feel that you've done enough for one time, put your letters or papers away and close the circle in your usual way. You can keep the things you've written for later study (in fact I recommend it), or you can destroy them if privacy is a worry.

If you wish, you can pick one or more of the feelings and possibilities you have outlined for later work. This ritual may bring some powerful emotions to the surface, and you should not be afraid to end the rite early if things are getting to be more than you can handle. There's no rush, and this ritual can be repeated as often as necessary. When you close the circle, put a pinch of incense on the coals in your burner or scatter a bit of bread or wine on the ground as an offering of respect and love for the Gods and a token of your will to heal the wound in your heart.

For other ritual work, Samhain is a good time for the remembrance of things we have left behind us. I also mark Samhain as the beginning of a period of meditation and self-examination leading up to the renewal of the year at Yule. This is a good time for ritual work devoted to the healing of grief wounds.

RECOMMENDED READING

Beck, Renee & Metrick, Sydney Barbara. *The Art of Ritual.* (Berkeley: Celestial Arts, 1990). A good guide to constructing rituals for dealing with all major life changes, including bereavement.

Clinebell, Howard. *Basic Types of Pastoral Care and Counseling: Resources for the Ministry of Healing and Growth..* (Nashville: Abingdon Press, 1984). This is an excellent reference for priests and priestesses who may have to help a circle member deal with loss. It is written from a Christian point of view, but it is not overbearing, and it can be easily generalized to a Pagan context.

Deits, Bob. Life After Loss: *A Personal Guide Dealing with Death, Divorce, Job Change and Relocation.* (Tucson: Fisher Books, 1988). Simply the best single book on the subject, in my opinion.

ABOUT THE AUTHOR

Paul Suliin is a priest of the Western Isian tradition of Wicca, a student of Ellen Cannon Reed and Chris Reed. Born in 1960, he has been a Witch for five years, coming to the Craft after several years as a ceremonial magician.

His articles have appeared in *Pagana*, *Enchanté*, and *Harvest*. He is a Pagan networker, deputy national coordinator of the Pagan/Occult/Witchcraft Special Interest Group of Mensa, and a member of the advisory board of the Alliance of Magical and Earth Religions.

Paul works as a chemist. He lives in Southern California with his wife, Michele, and their trained attack cat, Simon. He operates the Los Angeles Area Pagan Information Line and may be reached there at (310) 719-9097 or on CompuServe at UID 76366,3514.

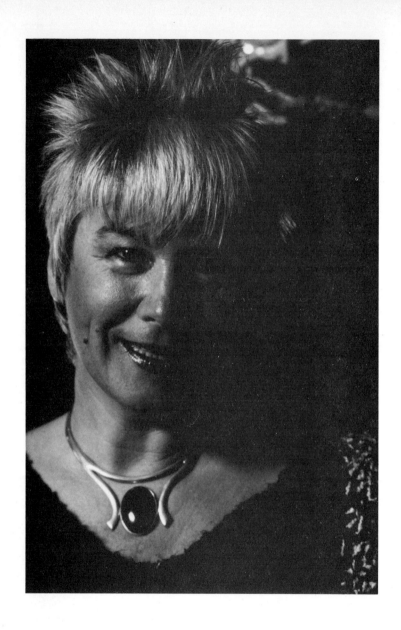

Z. Budapest
Photo © 1993 Malcolm Brenner / Eyes Open

Witches After 40

by Grey Cat

An edge crept into Amber Sky's voice as she glared across the room at Snow Wolf. "How can we do it that way?" she said. "You know that only Rebecca Spirit knows that part, and she isn't coming. Don't be such an idiot."

"If we can't discuss a simple ritual without your sinking to personal accusations, we certainly are going to have a hard time entering the circle with perfect love and perfect trust." Wolf glared at Amber and turned to Lugh with a slight smirk.

A group of coveners on the couch had their heads together in a cloud of whispers. Once again Ice Moon Coven was caught in a pointless argument. Perhaps this time dissension would tear the group apart.

As Amber opened her mouth to fire off her next salvo, a quiet knock sounded on the apartment door. "Get it," Lugh snarled at Green Beaver, the newest covener.

Through the timidly opened door a tall, slender woman crowned with a wildly curling halo of gray hair moved, smiling a rich, gentle smile. The room relaxed: Judith Lightstar was here, and everything would be all right. Moving to the big armchair, always left empty for her, Judith surveyed the group, noting the high color in the faces of the high priest and priestess. In her soft, loving voice she spoke into the respectful silence: "What is it, children?"

Is this an accurate picture of what we expect of a Craft elder? Not really, according to my survey of Witches over 40. They see themselves as dynamic forces both for change and for continuity with the past. They may not party as much as they used to (but party harder when they do, according to at least one), but they are more active in the Craft than ever before. Their concept of their roles as "elders" is focused outwardly toward the services they hope to offer the entire Wiccan community.

American Wicca includes individuals from all age groups, but population demographics being what they are, the crest of the curve is over the Baby Boomers, usually described as those people born from 1946–1964. The oldest "Boomers," of course, are now 45 or older. Five years ago, when I was about that age, I looked for role models both inside and outside the Craft, but most older women in both groups were quite taken up with the fight against the passing years.

I felt that in the majority culture a gap existed between perceptions of older women and older men. That sexually based gap, however, seemed less within the Craft because there, ironically, aging was perceived negatively whatever the sex of the "victim." As I considered the ways used in the majority culture to deny any status to the figure of the Crone, I realized that all the propaganda had the "smell" of fear to it. And when I consulted my own perceptions of my internal physical and mental changes, I concluded that they were wise to fear. The Crone is a scary figure in a real sense; it is logical that the "wicked old witch" figure so popular in late October is built upon her. Because she is "no longer a woman" (in other words, cannot bear children) but still not a man, the post-menopausal woman falls into that special category of "things between"—along with twilight, tidal flats, dew, and dreams between waking and sleeping. This is where magick dwells. A person holding within herself the state of "between" may be seen as intrinsically magical and powerful.

Respect for the elders of a community is found in societies as diverse of those of China, Africa, and pre-European America. Outside of the paternalistic societies of Europe, the Mediterranean, and India, respect for post-menopausal women is generally quite high. Partly because most of the really elderly individuals of a community at whatever level of civilization and/or medical care will be women, even societies such as that of old China that in general offered little respect and honor to females made the truly old woman the uncontested ruler of her household. Native Americans sought the wisdom of the Grandmothers and Grandfathers (some tribes using the terms as a method of honorable address without reference to blood relationships), and the wisdom sought from the Grandmothers was not more trivial or of less import than that sought from the Grandfathers.

Because even as Wiccans we share the majority culture's prejudices about aging, most of us are having to examine our own attitudes about it. As we reach these years, we are finding that we can take pride not just in our "wisdom" but in the lines that life and experience have graved in our faces, in the changed outlook that a longer perspective is giving us, and in the uninhibited enjoyment of the peculiar freedoms that age can bestow. No longer are we so concerned about how we appear to others; no longer are so many of our actions constrained by fears. We know that we can survive making a bad decision, that the enjoyment of relationships is worthwhile despite the possibility of later hurt, and that, while our actions have meaning and effect, the world will go on with or without us.

As I gradually came to these realizations, I suspected that other women (and their male counterparts) besides me existed who did not care to devote their energies to Oil of Olay or bouncing with Jane Fonda. Conscious of the population bulge which has followed close behind me all my life, I felt that exploring the positive aspects of aging as a Wiccan would allow me to make an important contribution to our religion.

Until recently, both male and female Witches tended to deny the fact of aging. Some of the emotional reaction to the Crone seems to be carried over (at least within the Craft) to older men too. The mainstream culture's concentration on youthful appearance was essentially repeated in the Craft, and Wiccans were expected to fight every year past 39.

I am not saying that attitudes have now changed totally nor that the whole leading edge of the Baby Boom cannot wait for the first gray hair. But it is now possible to find a good number of Wiccans who are not hesitant to admit to an age in excess of 40.

Much of Wicca has an initiatory degree system in

which the third-degree holder is considered an "Elder." However, the criteria for granting this degree focus usually on whether or not the person has the knowledge and skills to lead his or her own group and to teach students. Age and its associated wisdom are not necessarily required.

In preparing to write this article, however, I informally surveyed about two score Wiccans over the age of 40, mostly people whom I already knew. The survey was divided into two parts. The first explored experiences of persons whose Craft participation began after age 40:

1. Did you feel that too much of the First Degree training was spent on personal growth for your needs?

2. Did you feel that your experiences and accomplishments were given the respect and credit you feel you deserved?

3. Do you feel that you had expectations and/or needs that the usual training doesn't cover?

The questionnaire's second part addressed experiences of individuals over 40 who were active in the Craft:

4. What is an "elder"?

5. How do you feel about the tradition that a high priestess should retire when she reaches a certain age?

6. Do you find that your practice of the Craft has changed in the last ten or so years?

7. Do you find that you are becoming more involved in the "religious" aspects of Wicca and less in the "spellcraft" aspects?

8. Do you find that age and experience have brought you nearer something you could call wisdom?

9. Do you find people coming to you seeking answers because of their perception of elders as "the Wise"?

10. What proportion of your total time would you say you devote to the Craft?

11. What aspects of the Craft and/or priest/essing are you currently concentrating on?

12. What sorts of advice do you give to people getting ready to take advanced initiations?

13. Does your tradition have a ritual observing the passage from Mother to Crone? Father to Sage?

14. What do you see as the generalized role of older people in the Craft?

15. Has your level or style of participation in the Craft changed over the last few years?

16. Do you feel that we who are now the Elders are doing a good job of being role models for those multitudes behind us?

17. Do you see your age as an advantage in doing what you perceive as your work in the Craft?

18. Do you feel that you approach your age differently because you are Wiccan?

I received roughly 20 responses, ranging from brief answers to the questions to eight- or ten-page letters covering the topics the questions asked and more. Those who responded represented a variety of Wiccan traditions and included solitary practitioners, leaders of established conservative covens, and founders of new forms of Wicca. All in all, they agreed that something more than a third initiatory degree is required to earn the full title of Elder. They mentioned factors such as experience, wisdom, and age, for most felt that age indeed played an important part in the development of knowledge and wisdom and in gaining, as Zona Henderson of "The People" put it, "all the designs and persuasions."

Pete Pathfinder of the Aquarian Tabernacle Church in Washington state saw an element of Pagan community recognition in the term. "Eldership is first and foremost awarded by the community by its treatment of you and is always predicated upon your behavior, not upon your paperwork! Objectivity, reserve, careful consideration before acting, abandoning one's own 'best interests' in favor of the community's interests in your deliberations isn't always easy, but is a sure sign of maturity and what we have come to call Eldership. Other signs are the ability to tolerate other viewpoints cheerfully, to suffer fools gladly (to a point), to be the Warrior and lay down the rules for expected behavior in a way that they are honored and there is no need to become the fighting (read 'failed') Warrior, the ability to respond positively to the rules and expectations of others when in their sphere of influences, and clear perception of one's duty to the Gods and the great good of the religious movement."

M. Macha Nightmare, a California Witch, writes, "In 'native cultures'—and I use the term very loosely to mean, in general, ethnic cultures that have not been over-cultivated or which have not been too transformed from their origins by so-called civilization—age seems to be one necessary and indispensable characteristic of elder status (as the world 'elder' implies)."

While some of the people surveyed felt that "semi-retirement" from leading a coven or group was a desirable alternative for an Elder, the forced retirement of the priestess when she should cease to be "young and beautiful" (as advocated by Gerald Gardner in his 1950s books on modern Witchcraft) was acceptable only to one respondent. All others almost unanimously reacted with a brief, earthy expletive. Most felt, however, that many elders would choose to forego active day-to-day leadership in order to concentrate on other aspects of Wicca or because of physical limitations.

"Read literally," says Judy Harrow, author of this book's chapter on Pagans in the military, "that requirement is obviously age-ist nonsense. But I'm beginning to think that we indeed should retire from any *activity* that is getting to feel 'old' to us. Quitting before the energy peaks and turns 'downward' is the best way of preventing personal burnout and keeping our covens and other activities fresh. So, given a metaphoric reading, I find great wisdom in the tradition."

In fact, very few respondents had in any way retired from active leadership, and the list of areas currently absorbing their interest is varied and impressive. Due in part to Wicca's current spurt of growth, many are devoting time to organizational and administrative concerns. The growing number of groups which have achieved "church" status with state and federal governments and the number of priests and priestesses registered with state, city, and/or county governments has taken Wiccan leadership into the world of red tape, accountants, and tax deductions. (For more on this topic, see Pete Pathfinder's chapter on "Witchcraft and the Law" in book one of this series, *Witchcraft Today: The Modern Craft Movement.*) Consequently, service to the Wiccan community—and to the general community—takes many forms. Beyond the obvious direct services, these Elders design new ritual for public celebrations, actively network within Wicca through newsletters, speak to Wiccan and non-Wiccan groups, counsel, and write books and articles on the Craft. Many are concerned with new research, codifying their groups' knowledge, and leaving it as a legacy for those who will take up our wands.

Again, M. Macha Nightmare comments: "The traditional role of the elder is to pass on the heritage of the culture to future generations by teaching the young and by guiding the actions and decisions of the adults who are not yet elders to bring them into conformity with cultural norms. They are in a sense judges. Because Neopaganism is a new cultural development (and not centuries old as the diehard romantics among us claim), it is the role of Neopagan elders to, in effect, create our cultural heritage so that the survival of Neopaganism is ensured."

Michael Ragan, Ard File of the Temple of Danann, writes, "As an 'older' Wiccan, I feel an ever-increasing responsibility to the community as a whole. I think we need to be quicker to speak up at times when we see inequities. We need to take a stronger hand in trying to mold the Craft into a better movement. And it needs a lot of help. We need to emphasize the spiritual aspect more and the partying aspect less. We need to expose those who are self-aggrandizing and sating their own egos at the expense of others. We need to find ways of working around the factionalism. We need to stress the original 'Law' and throw away the paranoia of the Burning Times. We should concentrate on teaching the wisdom and forget 'keeping the secrets.'"

Several of us devote essentially all our work time to activity in the Craft. While all would agree with Lady Cybele that Wicca "'ain't no Sunday religion' and therefore 100 percent of our time can said to be devoted to Wicca," even the majority who must hold secular jobs devote up to 50 hours per week to Wiccan activities.

The 12 individuals who responded to this question with a concrete reference to hours put in a total of more than 500 hours per week or an average of 41.7 hours each.

Most described themselves as more involved with the religious aspects of Wicca than they were 10 years ago and feel that the Craft has changed during that time. Wiccans were seen as more secure, more responsible, more confident, and more public than before. Most were pleased that as a living religion Wicca is always changing and growing. Several thought that theology is an important area of Wiccan development. While one noted that some new groups lacked depth, a generally enthusiastic attitude toward the perceived changes refuted the old adage about "old dogs and new tricks."

While those who responded to my survey did not feel that attitudes towards age had changed much over the last ten years, they did feel that in general Wiccans have a more positive attitude towards older persons than does the popular culture. Moreover, more than half believe that being over 40 helps them in their work. All felt that they were wiser, although almost all "hope" their perceptions are accurate.

When I asked, "What do you see as the generalized role of older people in the Craft," I received a varied list of attributes and activities. Among them were writing and teaching; serving as a historian, particularly for perspective and a feeling of continuity with the past; and giving ethical guidance. Comparing the qualities of hypothesized, idealized Elders with the list I received, I concluded that indeed this group of Wiccans are concentrating on becoming the Elders that they have in the past imagined.

But there is also a downside to being an older Wiccan. Many of those responding mentioned that too few ritual organizers consider how to make large rituals and other group activities accessible to those with mobility problems. Like most other Wiccans, these Elders prefer when possible to hold their celebrations outdoors, but because the majority of individuals in the Craft fall into the "young and healthy" category, rarely is thought given to providing ways for those outside that category to participate. For instance, an outstanding failure to recognize this problem occurred at a leading Pagan festival in 1991 when a workshop on handicapped access was scheduled at a meeting site a quarter mile away from all campsites and up two steps as well! Festival attendance in general can be difficult for older persons. At the average Pagan gathering, participants find themselves doing a great deal of walking back and forth. In addition, sleeping on the ground, even in a tent, can be a real adventure in pain and stiffness for one whose joints lack the resiliency of youth.

I was surprised to learn that few respondents to my survey had or performed a special rite of passage to mark entry into true Eldership. In fact, one respondent had decided to do such a ritual, but in the end could not get others in her group to participate so it never happened. I have been helping to do "Croning" rituals for about five years, and all the reports I have received from those who have done such rituals have been very positive, indicating that a public observance of this transition was a highly positive experience.

Groups which have instituted or re-instituted puberty observances have not yet dealt with this next-to-last great life change. At this writing, I know of only three groups with a specific, separate ritual, although members of several others have shown recognition of its desirability. To further the development of a rite of passage into Eldership, I offer the ritual outline given below. It is adapted from the Croning ritual of North-Wind, an American Wiccan tradition. Ben Sharp and Pete Pathfinder contributed words and ideas during the original writing, and Wren's words were added at her Elden Ritual.

Finally, Wicca is reviving the old traditions of treasuring the elders' wisdom and experience. It falls upon those of us who are the first full generation of Crones and Sages in the Neopagan revival to fulfill our own goals and thereby break trail for the multitudes who follow.

Ritual of Eldership

The circle is cast according to group practice.

Maiden Priestess: *Brave Goddess, fair Diana, Huntress, Amazon, Corn Maiden, bringer of the sustaining bread, Goddesses of youth and energy, I call upon you to fulfill your pledges given of old. Grant me your grace and power to represent you in this Circle.* (Lights red Goddess candle.)

Mother Goddess Priestess: *Gentle Mother, Great Isis, Mighty Juno, Cerridwen of the Cauldron, Goddesses of care and nurture, I call upon you to bring your presence to your children here. Give to me your love and might to represent you in our rites this night.* (Lights blue Goddess candle.)

Crone Priestess: *Grandmother Hecate, who watches over the cauldron of Time, Grandmother Earth, wise women of Earth and Sky, old wise ones of the wisdom and justice, I call upon you, Ancient Ones. We peer beneath the veil in circle, where you stand at the North. The North Wind blows in your name to chill the heart yet nurture new life beneath the soil while turning the mind to contemplation. Give me your pity and strength to represent you in our rites tonight.* (Lights black or purple Goddess candle.)

Candidate: *Hecate hear me, Hecate attend me.*
  Give me wisdom that I may do what is needful.
  Give me strength that I may do it right.
  Give me compassion that I may do it only with good reason.
  Give me serenity that I may not be lost in pride.
  Hecate, be with me.

   Priest: *Mighty God of the golden Sun, the winter's cold, Odin the one-eyed, bringer of wisdom, Saturn the constrainer, melancholy Boreas, give your blessings and strength to this rite that we do in your names.* (Lights white God candle while the priestesses stretch out their hands showing their intended participation in the lighting. Short pause to get people comfortable.)

   Priest: *Lovely Lady, ardent Maiden, gentle Mother, dread-full Crone:* [name of candidate], *our companion here, wishes to present him/her-self for your special blessings. She/he comes to us under the call of the Crone to acknowledge becoming an EldMother/Father of the Wicca and to accept such duties as are appropriate to this station.*

Mother Priestess: *Do you*, [name], *seek the rights and duties of an EldMother/Father of your own free will and accord?*

Candidate: *I do.*

Crone Priestess: *Know now that it is not obligatory or automatic that you or anyone espouse the role of EldMother/Father. For such is a special summoning for those who are called to it by the Goddess.*

You whom the Crone Goddess summons to this third stage of wo/man must be a servant of all the community of the Wicca. You must be dedicated to the service of life in all the forms in which it manifests.

You must follow the path of peace and compassion, seek to relieve suffering in all its forms, and promote true spiritual growth in one and all, so that each may travel on his or her path. If you do these things and strive in these directions, then shall the Goddess and God grant to you a special measure of wisdom.

The wisdom of the Crone is granted to those who have come through blind faith, have passed by knowledge, and have had the courage to look their own death in the face. If you will strive to do these things, you will be known as Elder, EldMother/Father, Grandmother/Father, and Crone, and you shall have a special place in the hearts of the community and in the love of the Goddess and God.

Receive now, sister/brother, the oath of our Goddess the Crone, whose hands hold the threads of life and mystery of death and rebirth.

(Crone Priestess holds athame to oath-taker's breast.)

Will you, [name], seek always to know and to promote the will of the Goddess in all her phases, the Gods, and the community of the Wicca?

Candidate: *I will, the Goddess being my help.*

Crone Priestess: *Will you minister to the suffering of all who come to you, giving freely of your counsel according to the wisdom granted you?*

Candidate: *I will, the Goddess being my help.*

Crone Priestess: *Will you follow the path of peace and give freely when required of the wisdom granted you by the Goddess and God in all the councils of our community?*

Candidate: *I will, the Goddess being my help.*

Crone Priestess: *Will you support the practice of all the Wiccan tenets, espouse balanced life, and lend your special support to all who ask it?*

Candidate: *I will, the Goddess being my help.*

(Crone Priestess returns athame to altar.)

Maiden Priestess: *Now has our sister/brother heard and affirmed the charge of the Crone and of the Elder Gods. I call upon you, Dark Mother, Wise Woman, and Crone to grant to [name] a full mea-*

sure of your grace, to grant to him/her a special portion of your wisdom, and to dispose him/her to a compassionate heart and ready and willing hands.

Priest: *When it shall please you to summon him/her before you at the close of this life, I ask that you ease her/his passage and grant to him/her safe conduct to your Summerland.*

(Crone Priestess places both hands upon the candidate's head.)

Crone Priestess: *I call upon you and ask you, O Wise Hecate, here present in me, to give to him/her your blessings.*

(Now the Priest places both his hands atop the Crone Priestess's hands upon the candidate's head.)

Priest: *And those of Odin, he who brought wisdom to all people and the force and power of the North Wind, special guide and protector of this wo/man [name], to obtain for her/him all which she/he will now need as EldMother/Father to your honor and glory for her/him and for our community's benefit. I give him/her the grace, the blessing, and the wisdom of the Crone and of the Elder of the Gods.*

(Crone Priestess and Priest leave their hands in place. Maiden Priestess steps before the Candidate and places her hands upon the Priest's hands.)

Maiden Priestess: *Great Maiden, strong woman of youth and freedom, I who am you here in this circle call down upon our sister/brother [name] your energy and fire to your honor and glory for her/him and for our community's benefit. I bless you, [name], and give you the power of the Maiden Goddess.*

(All three leave their hands in place while the Mother Priestess steps before the Candidate and places her hands on his/her head also.)

Mother Priestess: *Mother of all, you who always care for us, I who am you here tonight call down your blessings and your loving care upon our sister/brother [name] to your honor and glory for her/him and for our community's benefit. I bless you, [name], and give you the feeling heart of Mother.*

Priest: *Welcome, EldMother/Father of the community of Wicca. Henceforth will your counsel be sought in the special deliberations of the community; now shall your door be open to those who seek your help. Your wisdom and aid are at the service of the whole Wiccan community, and a special place shall be accorded you in all the councils of the just.*

Candidate:
  Because I have seen through Her [His] eyes,
  Because I have spoken with Her [His, etc.]
    mouth,

Because I have loved with Her heart,
Because I have been Her,
I accept Her.
I am She.

I stand before the North Wind's door:
Her chill breath cleanses my soul,
Her dark wings enfold me,
Not dead, but dying, my eyes are clear.

(Priest faces outward to those attending the ritual.)

Priest: *I present unto you* [name], *who has received the blessings of our Lady Hecate and of Odin as Elder and EldMother/Father. She/he pledges himself/herself in the name of the three faces of the Goddess and of the Gods to serve all in our community. I pray you to receive her/him with understanding, with reverence, and with affection.*

Priestesses and Priest: *May the special blessings of the Gods and Goddesses be yours now and always.*

(Ground the circle in the group's customary manner, proceeding next to ritual meal and circle closing.)

ABOUT THE AUTHOR

Grey Cat came to Wicca in her early 40s. She trained under Michael Ragan of the Temple of Danann, an Irish tradition. Amber K, founder of Our Lady of the Woods and author of *True Magic* (Llewellyn Publications, 1990) shared much of the outline for her book and to this extent contributed to Cat's training.

In April 1988, Grey Cat founded NorthWind Tradition of American Wicca, which trains teachers and priest/esses. Her writing on Neopagan and Wiccan topics has appeared in *OPECNews, Circle Network News, Harvest, The Salamander, Covenant of the Goddess Newsletter, Wheel of Hecate,* and others. She edited *The Crone Papers* (rated in the top 10 in a *Green Egg* poll of Pagan publications). She is co-author of *American Indian Ceremonies: A Practical Guide to Medicine Path* (Inner Light Publications, 1989) and is currently working on a book about the methods and techniques of herbalism and on an anthology from *The Crone Papers.*

She also co-authored *Herbs for Magic and Medicine* with Michael Ragan and a Temple of Danann Correspondence course. She twice received the Silver Salamander Award for Excellence in Pagan Journalism. Grey Cat also wrote a chapter on "Witchcraft and Shamanism" for *Witchcraft Today Book One: The Modern Craft Movement,* Chas S. Clifton, editor (Llewellyn Publications, 1992).

Photo © 1993 Malcolm Brenner / Eyes Open

Pagan Rites of Dying

by Oz

Now seal the circle and dance and sing, And let my spirit pass through the ring; But don't worry, and don't you weep and mourn, 'Cause I been promised I'll be reborn. —Gwydion Pendderwen

Witches have always been associated in other peoples' minds with things fearsome and unknown, including death and the realms of the dead. Indeed, death, the underworld and the afterlife are not such strange places to Witches and those who regularly travel to such "otherworldly" places. Moving from one state of consciousness to another is our way of "walking between the worlds."

It is learning in this life how to transit from one reality to another, journeying into the astral realms, into our past lives, in and out of trances. It could be looked at as preparation for learning how to transit from life through death as well. On such journeys, we often have much discourse with "discorporate entities" (those without bodies). We talk with them, solicit their aid, and often have relationships with them much as we do with the living. This helps to dim the boundaries between the dead and the alive. My younger daughter once wisely commented that the wonderful thing about the Gods is that they don't care whether or not you are dead. This same open-minded attitude could be said to be held by many Neopagans, at least on a philosophical level.

Recently when I was speaking about the Craft on a call-in television talk show, one caller asked me to justify the Witches' celebration of Halloween, likening it to a worship of death. Her question itself belied an unspoken implication that any kind of relationship with death that was positive must be shameful and/or evil. Her attitude, which is that of most Westerners, demonstrated clearly a total contrast to that generally held by Neopagans. To answer her, I attempted to draw comparisons to the Japanese Shinto ancestral worship and honoring of their dead, or Mexico's great celebratory festival of "The Day of the Dead," which brings picnickers out to the cemeteries.

Sadly, although many intrinsically nature-oriented spiritualities which survive on this planet teach a healthy and enlightened attitude towards our own deaths and our own dead, they are today being seen more and more as bizarre and morbid oddities.

But just how deeply does the philosophical and experiential Neopagan approach to death and the otherworld affect our real lives, and deaths? How much does our familiarity with the beyond affect our relationship with and fear of death and dying? And our acceptance of the death of our loved ones? How does our approach to death and dying differ, and in what ways does this complicate our position in a world that relegates open discussions of our deaths to an even more socially unmentionable level than our sex lives? How do Witches handle death when it actually comes? Are we able to welcome this transition and celebrate the passing of a spirit, or do we too cower in fear as the specter with the sickle walks across our own shadows?

My first vivid experience with the death of a fellow Neopagan Witch was one that touched many in the burgeoning Pagan world very deeply. His name was Gwydion Pendderwen, and he was a man of great talent, widely known and much admired. He had begun a Pagan sanctuary in Northern California where he sponsored numerous large-scale tree plantings, and he had enchanted people at gatherings all around the country with his songs and "Faerie Shaman" magick. His music was the first Witches' music to be professionally recorded and distributed in this country, and he was known to many in other countries as well. He was a true Bard in the old ways, and when he died suddenly he left behind many a broken heart.

The loss dealt a blow of reality-shock to a mostly young community that had as yet not really faced its own mortality. Our first reaction was an incredible solidarity. Within hours, nearly everyone in the United States who knew, or knew of, Gwydion had received a phone call with the news. No one knows how many circles and ceremonies were held that very night or how many thousands of people joined in with songs to his soul and toasts to his life. Among the Pagans there was no burying our feelings or denial of the sense of loss. If anything, an outsider might have been amazed at what must have looked like a tremendous overreaction. We bonded together in our grief. Letters and phone calls poured in for months. Wakes were held again and again. Gwydion's songs were sung, and tales of his feats became more and more grandiose each time they were told. Legends about the "true" cause of his death arose, and everyone found words in his music and writings that showed he had foretold his own fate. It might have been a modern lesson in the manner in which the Welsh hero tales began. His life had sparked our imaginations, so perhaps it was fitting that this continue after his death.

However, Gwydion's death brought a great number of very practical questions, and along with the realities of handling the after-death situations came very important lessons.

Gwydion's death in an automobile accident was unexpected. He was quite rare among the relatively young in that he left a will and had discussed his post-death wishes with those who were close to him. In true Pagan earth-loving style, he had many times said he wanted to be buried under an oak tree on the mountain land that was his home, which he called Annwyn—the land of Forever Forests.

I went with Ayisha, who lived with Gwydion, to talk to his parents about his wishes. They were understanding and compassionate people, just like Gwydion himself. To them, he was still their son Tom, and it was important to honor his death in the ways familiar to them—with a good, normal, Christian funeral service. This was our first experience with what would later become a common conflict following the death of a Neopagan—the desires of the usually non-Pagan blood relatives versus the desires of the adopted Pagan family of friends.

Among his brothers and sisters of the Craft, many felt that we should fight for what we knew Gwydion would have wanted, and immediately research was begun for ways to set up a legal Pagan cemetery on the sanctuary land of Annwyn, legally incorporated under the Church of All Worlds. Being a church, however, did not make the process any easier. Morning Glory Zell did a lot of fast leg and brain work and found an incredible "Catch-22" in California state law. In the only legal precedent in that state, a private cemetery had been established on private land only by showing that it had been previously used for burial—some old gold miners' graves were found there. Apparently, we could only bury a body on our own land if another body had been buried there first.

We learned that cemeteries these days were not church or government entities, but in fact were business enterprises. As in many other private businesses, the system seemed stacked with red tape, effectively keeping out the minor competition. It looked rather more difficult to start a cemetery where we might bury our own dead that it would be to get a liquor license in a Mob-run neighborhood. Without establishing a cemetery, we couldn't bury a body where we wanted to. We had run up against a brick wall of realities, including other restrictions as to when, where, how, and why burial of a human could even take place. Suddenly we realized we were not only confronting a different set of beliefs and attitudes, but were up against years of acculturated, governmental, and financially developed systems that had neatly confined death practices into a set of traditions from which it was virtually impossible to depart.

Gwydion's parents suggested a compromise, offering to have Gwydion's body cremated and to give us the ashes to bury at Annwyn. We realized immediately that we were fortunate to reach an acceptable solution as easily as we did considering the constraints of time, emotions, and the two completely different world views that might well have clashed over the death of just one person.

The sobering experience of this death was a profound experience for those of us who felt ourselves on the leading edge of a religion's new growth. Suddenly we were faced with endless questions we had never before considered. Just what did we want to do before another one of us came close to death? What could we do about cemeteries, what about burials, and what about our respect for our genetic families versus our devotion to our own beliefs?

In the years since Gwydion's death, we have come to face many more realities about death and dying. The first situation I encountered had only to do with the after-death needs. Today, Pagans have also had to begin to learn what to do when we know that one of us is dying. The greatest nobility that I have seen yet among Pagans has been their willingness to confront and accept death. I once visited a Wiccan woman dying a slow death from breast cancer. She was surrounded day and night for months by her Pagan friends who volunteered to care for her so that she could die surrounded by her beloved cats and crystals. The care she was being given was spiritual as well as physical.

Once during preparations for a community Beltane rite, a woman my own age came to ask me if she could stand in the center when the energy was raised. "This may be my last, you know" she said, with a most sincerely joyous smile. I knew that she was dying, and I knew that she wanted to be part of the joy.

Those who knew her truly shared that day with her openly in celebration of life, with no apparent hint of sadness or fear.

Many of us have had our lives directly affected by the HIV virus, causing us to face and confront a great complexity of issues relating to a new era of potentially fatal conditions—personal, political, spiritual, and sexual. Nearly every Pagan community has experienced the angst of one or more of its loved ones succumbing to this often misunderstood illness, and in many cases has banded around the person in a show of support and acceptance. Our real selves have been challenged, yet everywhere Pagans are facing rather than avoiding the new issues of death that are penetrating our lives today. The presence of AIDS and other new diseases, along with mass generational aging, has brought a new constancy of awareness of death into our world. Our feelings, our relationships, and our choices have been permanently altered by our new familiarity with mortality.

This vivid presence of death in our midst has made us very conscious of death as a reality of the life cycle. Our new Pagan ways are based on a deep belief in the cycle of Life, Death, and Rebirth: the Wheel of Life. Everything in our eclectic, non-dogmatic, indefinable "liturgy" reflects this continuum. When we chant, we often say "There is no end to the circle, no end. There is no end to life, there is no end" (thanks to Starhawk). Or we sing "Hoof and horn, hoof and horn, all that dies must be reborn" (thanks again to Starhawk). Other chants, songs, and invocations speak of the grain or the corn being cut, dying, and growing again. Or the seed, which must die to germinate before it can grow into a new life. We sing about returning to the Goddess like a drop of rain returning to the sea and becoming one with the earth again. We celebrate the myth of Persephone journeying into the Underworld, the land of death. We invoke Hekate, the queen of death and rebirth.

All this reflects an undying belief in reincarnation and the evolution of the soul. Pagans disagree on most everything, but virtually every one of us adheres to a firm belief that the soul, the spirit, the consciousness, does not cease to exist when the body dies. Witches say that after death they will journey to a mystical place called "Summerland," a place of eternal beauty about which little is generally spoken. More often we hear of the promises of the Goddess having to do with the return to this life, the time of being reborn.

She says that the greatest of Her gifts to us is to cause us to be reborn again among fellow Witches, and preferably with those we have loved in this life. The cauldron we gather around is Cerridwen's, the cauldron of rebirth into which all souls must go and from which all new life issues. Our Goddess also reminds us constantly that everything changes, "that even death is not eternal."

As to what happens to the soul once it completes its cycles of incarnations, Witches are notably silent. Individual's personal interpretations of this mystery may be drawn from ancient mythologies, such as the Scandinavian or Tibetan. Traditionally, however, Pagans as earth-lovers seem much more concerned with the direct experience of that to which our earthly lives are closest. That exact connection between the spirit realm and the physical realm is the domain in which Witches tend to move and find their sense of strength. It is just because of this that there may be found so much courage and relative lack of fear when a

Witch or Neopagan is confronted by the reality of the transition through death.

For us, the veil between the worlds is, as they say, very thin. We do not see as much distinction between this life and the "other" life. Our frequent communications between these realms include conversations both with loved ones who have crossed over and a great variety of other spirit beings. The effects that the relative transparency of the life/death boundary has upon us are many. For one, Pagans often adhere to a belief that impending death is usually known beforehand by the person about to die—whether consciously or not. Messages indicating this may appear in dreams, omens, visions, or by direct knowing. In any "unexpected" death of a Witch or a Pagan, there is likely to be conversation afterwards about signs that foretold the coming fate.

Soon after his death, I went back and re-read Gwydion's most recent letters to me. Events in his last months left no doubt that his death was forthcoming, and that some part of him knew. He wrote to me of the day that a crow came and stole his personal magickal power ring. Just a few days later he found that the tree he called his "Life Tree" had died and fallen down. He knew something was happening, and he wrote much about it. Many people received communications from Gwydion after his death in the form of dreams, "synchronous" reminders and visual or auditory sensations. This is a completely common and expected phenomena to a Pagan, and as such simply strengthens our relative sense of comfort with our own approach to the afterlife.

Another effect our closeness to the beyond seems to create is a great fascination with those who have gone on, manifesting in a variety of unusually lingering feelings and actions surrounding our dead. Certainly, by our behavior one could interpret an especial attachment to the lives of our loved ones and to this earthly life.

Often it seems that it is exactly our redoubtable faith in the certainty of the afterlife and reincarnation which so strongly binds us to our dead. To us, those that have gone on are really not dead at all, and our emotional connections to them may remain as strong as in life. Thus our personal reactions to death, such as grief, anger, and the sense of loss, may be compounded by the very beliefs that also give us consolation.

When Gwydion died, I felt a tremendous sense of betrayal. We had once shared a vision in which we recalled having lived together in Scotland. In that life, we had vowed to carry on together what we believed to be an important spiritual and ecological mission. We felt that we had met in this life to fulfill this sacred vow. When his physical life ended, I felt cheated on a level that resonated in my soul. I could not understand how he could leave me again to carry on this work without his assistance. This sense of connection to others which transcends a single human lifetime makes "missing" one who has died rather different than grieving for one who is perceived as gone. It may be exactly because of this attitude that it is so difficult for us to say a very complete goodbye.

Sometimes, our dead live on with us in distinctive ways. A young Witch of our tradition literally dropped dead in his sleep one night, victim of a brain aneurysm. We, his Pagan family, were stunned. "Fuzzy Dan," as he was affectionately known because of his beard, became another deceased soul whose presence lingered on and on with those who cared for him.

In a compromise with his family, reminiscent of Gwydion, Dan was cremated and his ashes were given to his Pagan friends to do with as they saw fit. Dan quickly became known in this new incarnation as "Dusty Dan," and his ashes were divided into a nearly infinite number of small herb jars and film canisters and distributed among his many friends. After a series of moving and tearful Rites of Passage, wakes and ceremonies to honor Dan and scatter him, yet more of his remains continued to pop up at other ritual events for years. Just about the time the circle fire would be lit, someone would appear with a bit of "Dan Dust" to add to the ashes, and pronounce yet another eulogy.

"Never-ending Dan" eventually became in death a virtual metaphor on his lifelong habit of telling one too many shaggy-dog stories. Although it is heartening that Pagans so readily incorporate such humor into their ways of dealing with death, a situation like this also makes one wonder whether we are simply still searching for exactly what to do with our dead.

Unfortunately, for now, our death practices seem to be primarily compromises between the established customs of the society in which we live and our own desires to return to a more ecocentric manner of handling both the pragmatic tasks of body disposal and the process of spiritual acknowledgment and grieving. In most cases we would undoubtedly prefer both a ceremony and a burial that would be quite different from the current cultural norm. Yet Pagans are in a compromised position by the very nature of our religion, in that we as yet do not have the numbers or the status to effect vast changes in laws or customs. In time, we may be able to design the deliverance of our dead to be more appropriate to our beliefs, but for now the situations are often at best a trade-off. Some of us are being escorted out of this life very ceremoniously, yet via an unconventional blend of contrasting cultures. The funeral ceremony held for Gwydion by his parents was a classic instance.

The rite was held in the chapel of a funeral home. It was a rather large and churchy affair, with the usual huge baskets of fabric ferns and flowers, gothic-arched ceilings, and square pillars supporting the peaks. Dozens upon dozens of Gwydion's Pagan friends filed down the aisle, many dressed in their finest ceremonial garb or best medieval dress from the Society for Creative Anachronism. Clusters of people huddled near the coffin as some laid their hands upon Gwydion's hands and spoke to him loudly and emotionally.

A great number and assortment of people filled the room with an air of drama and discomfort, mixed with heavy grief and tangible sounds of wailing. It was a scene that would have done honor to a Monty Python film. In the front pew on one side of the chapel sat his mom and dad, brothers, aunts, and cousins. They were respectfully dressed in gray and black and sat subdued, with heads bowed. In the opposite front pew sat five women dressed in black fringe, scarves and velvets— his "widows." We wept loudly, hugging and consoling one another. We also spent much time tucking crystals into Gwydion's suit pockets and surreptitiously snipping locks from his beard and hair to save for talismans.

Gwydion's embalmed appearance in the open coffin looked incredibly odd. None of us had ever seen him in a suit before, and the dark, navy-blue clothing seemed like some sort of imposed punishment. His face was ashen white and stiff with makeup—so different from either life or what I knew to be the look of death. It all seemed like a dream. A large woman dressed in a flamboyant emerald satin Victorian gown shrieked up the aisle with her long flaming red hair streaming behind her. She collapsed before the coffin in heaving sobs. When the minister brought quiet, an incredible sense of both anachronism and anomaly prevailed.

Gwydion Pendderwen, beloved bard and priest of the Pagan world, was in this manner being "laid to rest." The minister began the service by saying that we were all gathered here to bid farewell to "Tom." I wondered how many people other than his family even knew that was his given name. When the minister wondered aloud what "Tom's" favorite Christmas carol might have been, there was a nearly audible cringe in the room. Gwydion was not fond of the Christianized versions of ancient Yule songs.

After the service the widows approached the funeral director and asked that Gwydion please be dressed in his shaman's robes for the cremation. We were never sure whether or not that actually happened, but our attempt to add what we thought of as dignity to his last passing was all we could do. How much I wished at that moment that we could have dressed and cared for the body that we had loved in life and laid it into the earth ourselves.

In an effort to establish our own meaningful and personal traditions, we are often compelled to create, or re-create, our own rites as they are needed. Gwydion did ultimately receive his request to be buried under an oak tree. A few weeks after the unfitting first funeral, a Pagan ceremony was held in a beautiful clearing on his home land of Annwyn. His ashes were put into the earth inside a handmade pottery urn, and 13 redwood trees were planted in a giant ring around him. Beside the baby oak which was planted over the grave was built a manzanilla-wood altar upon which were placed many gifts and talismans as reminders both of what he meant to us in life and what we hoped for him in his own ongoing journey. The many people who attended his Pagan burial came each to give salutations in their own way. Creativity definitely prevailed.

The rite was begun with children running around the perimeter of the circle tossing brussels sprouts away to the outside. To Gwydion, brussels sprouts were the most repulsive of all natural creations, and thus were deemed a fitting "exorcism" symbol for his ritual purification. Many people spoke, both in beautiful poetical tributes and in moving spontaneous words. Many placed personal tokens in the earth alongside his ashes to serve as blessings for Gwydion. Several drafts of whiskey were poured on the ground in a more typically Celtic tribute. The ritual was a thing of beauty—beautiful people gathered in a place of stunning natural beauty, beautifully dressed and speaking beautiful words. The last physical remains of Gwydion were placed where everyone knew his heart would always be, partly in hopes that something of him would remain on this sacred land that he made to be a natural haven for others.

Pagan rites of passage are marked by their moving beauty and informal "real-ness," as well as a focus on healing for the spirit of the deceased and the ones who mourn. A ceremony used in my home circle borrows traditional healing concepts from several sources. The first time we performed this ceremony, we had no body or ashes since the family took the young woman to her home state for burial. We used instead an earthen clay vessel to symbolize her body. Into this vessel we placed water, to represent the waters of life. We also put in bits of Melanie's hair and her favorite ring, to charge the vessel as a living link to her. Melanie's lover carried this vessel to a circle that we formed beside the Rio Grande. We invoked Melanie's spirit into the circle, and each person spoke to her, saying whatever it was they wished to say before we released her fully into the spirit realms.

Each person stepped forward in the dark night to a small fire of glowing coals in the center of the ring and spoke aloud to Melanie's spirit. There was a tremendous outpouring of tears and grief in a wonderful catharsis of relief and healing. Words that were spoken were in no way a simple repetition of spiritual platitudes. These were words from hearts heavy with unsuppressed grief. Children wept and spoke to Melanie of their feelings of loneliness. Her closest friends forgave her for hurts that had not been healed. Many thanked her for specially shared moments and insights that had been important in both lives, hers and theirs.

Then Melanie's vessel was carried to the edge of the river and broken into pieces to symbolize the expiring of her body. As the water and the broken pieces were swept away by the river's current, we felt her presence sail away from the circle. She was released to rejoin the flow of all Spirit. Bells were rung to symbolize her rebirth in the world beyond as these words were spoken:

> *We come to this circle to bid farewell to our beloved friend, to give her over to the care of the Goddess and the God of the Ancients that she may rest, free from illusion or regret, until her rebirth. And knowing this is so, we know also that sadness is earthly, but that joy is all. As there is reason for being here in this world, so there is reason to journey beyond to the peace of the world of eternal summer and joy—the place standing between life*

and life. Happiness and renewed youth are there. Great Ones, we sadly yet joyfully give over our friend. Take her, guard her, guide her— bring her in the fullness of time to a new birth and a new life. And grant that in that new life she may be loved again, as we her sisters and brothers have loved her here.

We stood that night, in the light of a nearly Full Moon, watching the water of the river rush by, holding one another and chanting, as much for ourselves as for her:

> *Everything lost is found again, in a new form, in a new way. Everything hurt is healed again, in a new life, in a new day.*

Wherever Melanie's body was, I did not know. But I was sure that I saw her spirit that night, disappearing down the line of that river into the stars on the southern horizon.

The way in which our preferred rites contrast with the common rites of modern Western society reflects the entire difference between indigenous beliefs and the beliefs of those who have largely handed their faith over to institutions. Many Pagans would actually prefer to touch and care for the body of the loved one than to leave this work to others. Just so, we much prefer our experiential and emotional ceremonies to a formal speech that is often delivered by a minister who never even knew the person who has died.

Much of society delegates what they see as the unpleasant tasks of death to impersonal professionals. This has taken everything about death out of our homes, and thus out of our lives. Death has become even more unknown and feared. The general Western attitude about dying is that it makes a person's body and their consciousness become immediately untouchable. In the ancient and traditional ways, this is not so, and it is not our way. Today's Pagans, like all other worshippers of nature, value ceremonies that touch and aid the spirit both in preparing for and following death. We do not want to look the other way when death comes.

A Pagan's acceptance of death may be enhanced by the experience of traditions that honor an ongoing connection to the dead, such as observed in today's Wiccan celebration of Samhain, or Halloween. The roots of this festival may be traced back to the Egyptian Feast of Osiris, and to the Celtic celebration of the dead from which we take the name Samhain. In the Samhain circle the living and the dead are brought as close as possible. Souls of departed friends and families are invited to be part of the ritual, to commune, speak, share and join in the feasting. Here, it is said, life and death meet and make one. Here we seek to reunite rather than separate the wholeness of existence, much as the diverse worlds converge in dreams and shamanic journeys. In this way, we maintain an awareness of the place to which we each will eventually journey, and in so doing we are able to be more at peace with our thoughts about this destination.

And yet, there is so much more to be addressed about death and dying. Our ways of preparing for death are evolving from our interdimensional explorations, our involvement with dying, and our years of experience in the sacred ceremonial circle. Some of us have become wise enough to see the practical need for wills and have begun to think about our burial preferences and our legal options. Those of us who are living must address this while we are alive, or leave it to become an issue between our families and friends after we are gone. If we want to see changes, we must take the responsibility to create them.

Before I learned the lessons of Gwydion's death, I had always said that when I died I wanted to be buried in the garden where I might decompose like compost and become food for the flowers and vegetables. A friend of mine who is a Cherokee chief had told me of his people's belief that the soul is not totally freed until the body is completely decomposed. I thought then of sterile embalmed bodies lying in fiberglass coffins in cement- and plastic-lined waterproof graves. After a conversation with a lawyer in my home state, I decided to write a will and specify my wish to be placed naturally in the earth. While this goes against many health regulations, there is a law in my home state of New Mexico that says a person's burial wishes must be followed if stated in the will. I decided it was time to test this law.

There are as well many moral questions about dying that members of our religion must consider. Individual decisions need to be made about the right to choose death rather than medical heroics, living wills, and even assisted suicide. Historically, Witches have been healers. Our potions and herbal wisdoms have helped us stay in charge of both our own lives and deaths. We have had the wisdoms to bring conception when it is desired, and have always known natural ways to terminate unwanted pregnancy. We have worked spells and rites to heal and save lives, but every true Witch's cauldron could also contain the poison that would bring a swift and sure death if desired.

For people who once lived close to the earth and breathed both life and death in every day, such wisdoms are only extensions of natural human birthrights and the cycles of nature. It seems to be one of our tasks to restore ancient wisdoms pertaining to our human destinies in the age of technology and mass urbanization. And perhaps the most important of all is the knowing of the absolute sacredness of all human life, and death.

In our rites, we affirm this sacredness of life, and of death and rebirth. In our lifetimes we honor the joy of being alive, and celebrate our faith in the continuation of this life past the time of death. This is intrinsic to our religion, and a foundation of today's Paganism. As Neopagan traditions are being written and remembered, we are in a process of newly developing rites and ceremonies that honor our unique approach to death, both literally and figuratively. Our willingness to meet death combined with our recognition of the power of ceremony is bringing about bold new concepts in both rites for those who have died and for those who are about to die—which, in reality, is every one of us.

We work our ceremonies to release the spirit and to heal the grieving. Recently some of us have also seen the need for a ceremonial process that brings us consciously into a spiritual readiness for death. It is said that the purpose of the ancient Pagan Eleusinian mysteries was to grant the initiate freedom from fear of death. We know that the symbol which was shown to the candidate who succeeded through the trials of these rites was an ear of grain, that selfsame symbol of rebirth of which we often sing in our chants.

There is a great lesson herein for today's world. It may be that our mysteries once held the knowledge of a way to approach death that far transcends anything which we retain in our spiritual repertoire today. As we open ourselves to a true spiritual approach to death, we may find ourselves challenged to relearn this wisdom. As death is becoming such a presence to us, now is the time to take another look. There may be skills to be restored, ways to make our deaths more spiritually conscious experiences, avenues leading us through that transition with a strength and readiness.

We are the developing generation of a religion based on deep roots in the past and coming of age during a renaissance of technologically stimulated communications between all races on this planet. We are in a unique position. The beliefs of Wicca are very ancient, yet our spokespersons are very much of this age. Already we are seeing that, simply because of its mass, this generation is shaping revolutions in consciousness as it moves through the phases of life. When we became old enough to have babies, we overthrew the medically dominated paradigm for a return to "natural" childbirth. The Witches, who were also once the midwives, were there. We are already beginning to face the actual deaths of our parents and friends, and we have only begun to see the changes that the dying process will surely undergo in the next generations. Many of the Goddesses worshiped by Neopagans are midwives, not only for birth but also for the transition of dying. Some of the Gods we worship are those who accompany the soul on its journey out of this world and into the next. These may be our teachers, but we are also looking around us at the real-life experience of dying to see what this can teach us. For many Pagans, familiarity with and open acceptance of death may be our guide to personally liberated dying. Through this open-eyed approach, we may also ultimately help others around us approach the end of their lifetimes with a renewed and supported conscious awareness.

None of us can ever really know how to die. No philosophy or psychic practice will completely prepare us. There is no practice for death, except perhaps in living life itself. If we hope to make a better entry into the next world, we simply need to learn as much as we can about ourselves. Lessons about dying are all around us. The cycle of life, death, and rebirth never ceases, whether in seeds or animals or humans or Gods. Our best way to learn is to ever be more a part of the process rather than apart from it. Neopagans are especially suited to this task. The Neopagan approach to life is typically a hands-on, get down and into it savoring of all sensations and experiences. I try to imagine what will happen if we take the same approach to death that we have to living. Dying will never be the same again.

My feelings about death were forever changed in my first close encounter. My grandfather gave me the gift of this lesson in how to die. He was not a Witch, but in his own way he was something of a Neopagan, for he had lived with the Native American people and subscribed to a Rosicrucian philosophy. When it came time for him to die, he chose to do so consciously. He was ready, and faced it as the next appropriate step in what he felt was a full life. He lay in the bed in his own home as I helped to care for him in his last days. Friends came from as far away as neighboring states to say goodbye, and he responded cheerfully to every one of them.

As death approached, I sat holding his hand and empathically feeling what his body and spirit were going through in their attempt to separate. I felt his whole being struggling to free his soul from his body. His face and the sense of his will were totally familiar to me, for they were the same expressions and same non-physical sensations that I had experienced when I was in labor giving birth to my children. It was as though every bit of him psychically struggled to push his consciousness out of that body in the same way I had recently labored to force an independent consciousness out of my body. He was giving birth to his own freed soul. The feeling was so startlingly vivid that I knew in that moment, absolutely beyond doubt or fear, that to die is literally to be born again.

(The La Caldera Foundation has been formed to study and develop alternative ceremonial practices for preparation for death, the dying process, and after-death rites. Interested persons may write in care of 211 12th St NW, Albuquerque, New Mexico 87102.)

STAY IN TOUCH

On the following pages you will find some of the books now available on related subjects. Your book dealer stocks most of these and will stock new titles in the Llewellyn series as they become available. We urge your patronage.

To obtain our full catalog, to keep informed about new titles as they are released and to benefit from informative articles and helpful news, you are invited to write for our bimonthly news magazine/catalog, *Llewellyn's New Worlds of Mind and Spirit*. A sample copy is free, and it will continue coming to you at no cost as long as you are an active mail customer. Or you may subscribe for just $10.00 in the U.S.A. and Canada ($20.00 overseas, first class mail). Many bookstores also have *New Worlds* available to their customers. Ask for it.

Llewellyn's New Worlds of Mind and Spirit
P.O. Box 64383-378, St. Paul, MN 55164-0383, U.S.A.

* * *

TO ORDER BOOKS AND TAPES

If your book dealer does not have the books described, you may order them directly from the publisher by sending full price in U.S. funds, plus $3.00 for postage and handling for orders *under* $10.00; $4.00 for orders *over* $10.00. There are no postage and handling charges for orders over $50.00. Postage and handling rates are subject to change. We ship UPS whenever possible. Delivery guaranteed. Provide your street address as UPS does not deliver to P.O. Boxes. UPS to Canada requires a $50.00 minimum order. Allow 4-6 weeks for delivery. Orders outside the U.S.A. and Canada: Airmail—add retail price of book; add $5.00 for each non-book item (tapes, etc.); add $1.00 per item for surface mail.

FOR GROUP STUDY AND PURCHASE

Because there is a great deal of interest in group discussion and study of the subject matter of this book, we offer a special quantity price to group leaders or agents. Our Special Quantity Price for a minimum order of five copies of *Witchcraft Today, Book Two* is $29.85 cash-with-order. This price includes postage and handling within the United States. Minnesota residents must add 6.5% sales tax. For additional quantities, please order in multiples of five. For Canadian and foreign orders, add postage and handling charges as above. Credit card (VISA, MasterCard, American Express) orders are accepted. Charge card orders only ($15.00 minimum order) may be phoned in free within the U.S.A. or Canada by dialing 1-800-THE-MOON. For customer service, call 1-612-291-1970. Mail orders to:

LLEWELLYN PUBLICATIONS
P.O. Box 64383-378, St. Paul, MN 55164-0383, U.S.A.

Prices Subject to Change Without Notice

WITCHCRAFT TODAY, BOOK ONE
The Modern Craft Movement
edited by Chas S. Clifton

For those already in the Craft, and for those who stand outside the ritual circle wondering if it is the place for them, *Witchcraft Today 1* brings together the writings of nine well-known Neopagans who give a cross-section of the beliefs and practices of this diverse and fascinating religion.

The contributors live in cities, small towns and rural areas, from California to Ireland, and they have all claimed a magical birthright—that lies open to any committed person—of healing, divination, counseling and working with the world's cycles.

Written specifically for this volume, the articles include:
• "A Quick History of Witchcraft's Revival" by Chas S. Clifton
• "An Insider's Look at Pagan Festivals" by Oz
• "Seasonal Rites and Magical Rites" by Pauline Campanelli
• "Witchcraft and Healing" by Morwyn
• "Sex Magic" by Valerie Voigt
• "Men and Women in Witchcraft" by Janet and Stewart Farrar
• "Witches and the Earth" by Chas S. Clifton
• "The Solo Witch" by Heather O'Dell
• "Witchcraft and the Law" by Pete Pathfinder Davis
• "Witchcraft and Shamanism" by Grey Cat
• "Being a Pagan in a 9-to-5 World" by Valerie Voigt

Also included are additional resources for Wiccans including publications, mail order suppliers, pagan organizations, computer bulletin boards and special-interest resources. The Principles of Wiccan Belief are also restated here.

0-87542-377-9, 208 pgs., 5 1/4 x 8, softcover **$9.95**

BUCKLAND'S COMPLETE BOOK OF WITCHCRAFT
by Raymond Buckland

Here is the most complete resource to the study and practice of modern, non-denominational Wicca. This is a lavishly illustrated, self-study course for the solitary or group. Included are rituals; exercises for developing psychic talents; information on all major "sects" of the Craft; sections on tools, beliefs, dreams, meditations, divination, herbal lore, healing, ritual clothing and much, much more. This book unites theory and practice into a comprehensive course designed to help you develop into a practicing Witch, one of the "Wise Ones." It is written by Ray Buckland, a very famous and respected authority on Witchcraft who first came public with the Old Religion in the United States. Large format with workbook-type exercises, profusely illustrated and full of music and chants. Takes you from A to Z in the study of Witchcraft.

Never before has so much information on the Craft of the Wise been collected in one place. Traditionally, there are three degrees of advancement in most Wiccan traditions. When you have completed studying this book, you will be the equivalent of a Third-Degree Witch. Even those who have practiced Wicca for years find useful information in this book, and many covens are using this for their textbook. If you want to become a Witch, or if you merely want to find out what Witchcraft is really about, you will find no better book than this.

0-87542-050-8, 272 pgs., 8 1/2 x 11, illus., softcover $14.95

THE FAMILY WICCA BOOK
The Craft for Parents & Children
by Ashleen O'Gaea

Enjoy the first book written for Pagan parents! The number of Witches raising children to the Craft is growing. The need for mutual support is rising—yet until now, there have been no books that speak to a Wiccan family's needs and experience. Finally, here is *The Family Wicca Book*, full to the brim with rituals, projects, encouragement and practical discussion of real-life challenges. You'll find lots of ideas to use right away.

Is magic safe for children? Why do some people think Wiccans are Satanists? How do you make friends with spirits and little people in the local woods? Find out how one Wiccan family gives clear and honest answers to questions that intrigue pagans all over the world.

When you want to ground your family in Wicca without ugly "bashing;" explain life, sex, and death without embarrassment; and add to your Sabbats without much trouble or expense, *The Family Wicca Book* is required reading. You'll refer to it again and again as your traditions grow with your family.

0-87542-591-7, 240 pgs., 5 1/4 x 8, illus., softcover $9.95

ANCIENT WAYS
Reclaiming the Pagan Tradition
by Pauline Campanelli, illus. by Dan Campanelli

Ancient Ways is filled with magick and ritual that you can perform every day to capture the spirit of the seasons. It focuses on the celebration of the Sabbats of the Old Religion by giving you practical things to do while anticipating the sabbat rites, and helping you harness the magical energy for weeks afterward. The wealth of seasonal rituals and charms are drawn from ancient sources but are easily performed with materials readily available.

Learn how to look into your previous lives at Yule . . . at Beltane, discover the places where you are most likely to see faeries . . . make special jewelry to wear for your Lammas Celebrations . . . for the special animals in your life, paint a charm of protection at Midsummer.

Most Pagans and Wiccans feel that the Sabbat rituals are all too brief and wish for the magick to linger on. *Ancient Ways* can help you reclaim your own traditions and heighten the feeling of magick.

0-87542-090-7, 256 pgs., 7 x 10, illus., softcover $12.95

THE URBAN PAGAN
Magical Living in a 9-to-5 World
by Patricia Telesco

Finally, a book that takes into account the problems of city-dwelling magicians! When preparing to do ritual, today's magician is often faced with busy city streets and a vast shortage of private natural space in which to worship. Technology surrounds, and fear and misunderstanding still exist about "magic" and "witchcraft." This leaves even experienced spiritual seekers trying desperately to carry a positive magical lifestyle into the 21st century. With the help of *The Urban Pagan*, we all can learn to incorporate earth-aware philosophies of days gone by with modern realities.

The Urban Pagan is a transformational book of spells, rituals, herbals, invocations and meditations that will help the reader to build inner confidence, create a magical living environment, and form an urban wheel of the year. It updates interpretations of symbolism for use in sympathetic magic and visualization, shows how to make magical tools inexpensively, provides daily magical exercises that can aid in seasonal observances, shows practical ways to help heal the earth, and explains the art of cultivating and using herbs, plus much, much more.

0-87542-785-5, 336 pgs., 6 x 9, illus., softcover $13.00

WICCA
A Guide for the Solitary Practitioner
by Scott Cunningham

Wicca is a book of life, and how to live magically, spiritually, and wholly attuned with Nature. It is a book of sense and common sense, not only about Magick, but about religion and one of the most critical issues of today: how to achieve the much needed and wholesome relationship with out Earth. Cunningham presents Wicca as it is today: a gentle, Earth-oriented religion dedicated to the Goddess and God. This book fulfills a need for a practical guide to solitary Wicca—a need which no previous book has fulfilled.

This book presents the theory and practice of Wicca from an individual's perspective. This book, based on the author's nearly two decades of Wiccan practice, presents an eclectic picture of various aspects of this religion. Exercises designed to develop magical proficiency, a self-dedication ritual, herb, crystal and rune magic, recipes for Sabbat feasts, are included in this excellent book.

0-87542-118-0, 240 pgs., 6 x 9, illus., softcover $9.95

LIVING WICCA
A Further Guide for the Solitary Practitioner
Scott Cunningham

Living Wicca is the long-awaited sequel to Scott Cunningham's wildly successful *Wicca: a Guide for the Solitary Practitioner.* This new book is for those who have made the conscious decision to bring their Wiccan spirituality into their everyday lives. It provides solitary practitioners with the tools and added insights that will enable them to blaze their own spiritual paths—to become their own high priests and priestesses.

Living Wicca takes a philosophical look at the questions, practices, and differences within Witchcraft. It covers the various tools of learning available to the practitioner, the importance of secrecy in one's practice, guidelines to performing ritual when ill, magical names, initiation, and the Mysteries. It discusses the benefits of daily prayer and meditation, making offerings to the gods, how to develop a prayerful attitude, and how to perform Wiccan rites when away from home or in emergency situations.

Unlike any other book on the subject, *Living Wicca* is a step-by-step guide to creating your own Wiccan tradition and personal vision of the gods, designing your personal ritual and symbols, developing your own book of shadows, and truly living your Craft.

0-87542-184-9, 208 pgs., 6 x 9, illus., softcover $10.00

Prices Subject to Change Without Notice